DENIS DIDEROT

DIALOGUES

DIALOGUES

BY

DENIS DIDEROT

Translated with an Introduction
by Francis Birrell

CAPRICORN BOOKS
NEW YORK

CAPRICORN BOOKS EDITION 1969

PRINTED IN THE UNITED STATES OF AMERICA

INTRODUCTION

By SIR EDMUND GOSSE, C.B., LL.D.

FRENCH LITERATURE IN THE EIGHTEENTH CENTURY

Every generation approaches the history of literature with fresh eyes, revising the judgments of the past and recapitulating its own prejudices. In the course of a hundred and fifty years there have been many changes of critical opinion with regard to the product of the Eighteenth Century. In the heyday of romanticism it was attacked with contemptuous fury as though it had been another Bastille. It was not a period of sensibility or imagination, and when nothing else than lyric passion was valued in literature, the masters of so calm an epoch were left out in the cold. We have entered into a new phase, and each decade which divides us from the Revolution offers us opportunities of contemplating the Eighteenth Century in better perspective. We see a period in some respects unique in human history; following an age of force which had hardened into austerity, preceding an age of revolt when all the ideals and traditions were broken, the Eighteenth Century appears like a strip of meadowland between cliffs and the sea. It is, to pursue the image, a field which is flat and at its edges sandy, but on which there flourishes a profusion of flowers. Across this tract there is a marked division; its upper half is hard and dry, diversified by a few monuments marked with the names of Buffon, Montesquieu, Saint Simon, Voltaire. Through its lower half creeps a river, Rousseau, neither swift nor clear, but spreading prodigal moisture in all directions, and encouraging a tangle of lush growths. This marish of sentimentalities and social contrasts leads us down to the ocean of 1789.

By common consent, Bayle is recognized as the father of the Eighteenth Century, though he hardly entered it. But it was he who started that restless intellectual vitality, often expending itself in mere vivacity, which was its characteristic feature. Bayle was a man who eschewed the dogmatic attitude, to whom everything was a question, who insisted on liberty of the intellectual conscience. Released by the death of Louis XIV from her burden of dogma, France stretched her arms and breathed anew. She changed her fashions, she adopted new formulas, she spoke of "progress," of "liberty," of "tolerance"—unfamiliar things. The earliest exhibition of the new sense in literature was the acceptance of modern aims in writing. The tyranny of the Ancients, which had long been resisted, was finally cast off. Madame Dacier, in her translation of the *Iliad* (1699), took the liberty of changing whatever in Homer she believed would offend French taste. The Abbé Terrasson, charged with erudition, decided after long comparison that Tasso was far superior to Homer as a poet. The first act of the Eighteenth Century was to cut itself off from the discipline of antiquity.

On the space thus left vacant it began to build its graceful and convenient structures. There was no violent breach between the old style and the new. The poets, such as they were, still were pastoral, but they gave their shepherdesses the tone of polished society, and taught them to sigh with elegance. Wit took the place of passion, because refinement must be cultivated in a purely modern society. To sparkle was the one thing essential. Whatever qualities the authors of a polite age may have, "il faut qu'ils aient de l'esprit, et de l'esprit fin et galant." The Great Age had been sublime, but its majesty had concealed much roughness and commonness. These could hardly be removed without an effort, to which the Marivaux and La Chaussées were manifestly unequal. Elegance, however, must at all costs be attained, and all that could be done was to veil the coarseness of manners with pink gauze. Pathos examined itself in the mirror, and rearranged its costume. Even the author of *L'Esprit des Lois* wrote *Le Temple de Guide*, and declared that "il n'y a que des têtes bien frisées et poudrées qui connaissent tout le mérite" of the new psychology.

Among the changes which followed the accession of Louis XV, none was more remarkable than the complete decay of theological ardour. The psychology of the great preachers whose eloquence had ruled French prose in the seventeenth century wholly evaporated. Gay revellers galloped over the prostrate statue of Bossuet, and it needed stronger arms than those of Massillon to keep them at bay. That graceful religious moralist was the last of the preachers, the only survivor of a giant race. But he was as innocuous as he was pious, and Voltaire could, without disturbance, enjoy having Massillon's sermons read aloud to him when he dined alone. If theology declined, science took its place. That embracing genius, Buffon, instructed an eager world in a new passion, the love of natural objects. The Eighteenth Century, having thrown off all illusions about human nature, was obliged to endow animals and plants, and presently lakes and mountains, with endearing and imaginary qualities. In this, as in much else, England served as a lighthouse, by which taste was steered in the night. England to the Eighteenth Century was the fortunate island, the one state in which thought was free. Her moral philosophy was seductive, and not Shaftesbury alone, but Mandeville and even Collins had his French disciples. Landscape, through Pope's convention and Thomson's realism, filtered into the intellectual scene, upon which the effect of the English novelists, particularly of Richardson, was immense. *Clarissa* continued to be the most influential of novels until *La Nouvelle Héloïse* diverted sentimentality into a wider channel.

The influence of polite society on literature was paramount in the Eighteenth Century, when it reached an ascendency in France which has been seen nowhere else. Typical of the age is the famous portrait of Mme de Pompadour by La Tour; she sits, dressed in the height of fashion, in a delicate boudoir, with a folio volume of the *Encyclopédie* in front of her, the goddess of philosophedom. Earlier, the same marvellous La Tour had painted the Duchesse du Maine, as the supreme law-giver of literature, in her academical palace of Sceaux, that temple of the arts. It is in the pastels of the artists that we read the full refinement of the age, when books were written to stimulate and to please, while the one unpardonable sin was to be crude. The sportive gallant century romped and fiddled to its close, taking on dolphin-colours after the deaths of Voltaire and Rousseau in 1778. Its highest point had been reached in the days of its comparative sobriety, before the delicate ethics of Vauvenargues had succumbed under the pressure of the sentimentalists, and before the relaxation of manners had culminated in the boudoir story. But it was all consistent. From Fontenelle to Diderot, under many forms, the spirit of the Eighteenth Century remained coherent, doubtless with a more subtle unity than can be met with elsewhere in the history of the mind. This individuality gives its literary history in France a peculiar interest, and, for those who are not by temperament averse to its neatness and dryness, an essential charm.

To LUDMILLA PITOËFF

Il y a plaisir à causer avec vous. Vous ne saisissez pas seulement, ce qu'on vous dit : vous en tirez encore des conséquences d'une justesse qui étonne.

DOCTEUR BORDEU.

Clive, Sir, is a nice thing to sit by. She understands what you say.

DOCTOR JOHNSON.

Let us accept things as they are. Let us find out how much they cost us and what we get for our money. And let us leave on one side all those things we do not understand sufficiently well to be able either to blame or praise them, and which perhaps are, as many intelligent persons think, neither good nor bad, but merely inevitable.

LE NEVEU DE RAMEAU.

CONTENTS

Dialogues of Denis Diderot

INTRODUCTION

I

WHEN the sculptor Falconet started forth to Russia to swell the diapason of Great Catherine, he sent home his *impressions de voyage* to his friend Diderot in Paris, who replies to one observation:

"I am delighted, though not in the least surprised, to learn that the Jews of Berlin are less disagreeable than has been reported."

This characteristic reaction to a piece of traveller's chatter, trifling as may be the occasion of it, sums up the charm of Diderot. Never was there a writer with so little nonsense about him, with so few repressions, angularities, jealousies, vanities, and hatreds. His good nature and good spirits beam out through all his writings. At the end of reading him, we love the man, and are not pleased to be reminded of his limitations, of his bad taste, his sentimentality, his frequent muddle-headedness, his general absence of imagination. Here he is unique among the great writers of his generation. Attempts to sentimentalize Voltaire, though frenzied and frequent, have hardly been successful. Rousseau, though possessing many qualities Diderot lacked, was admittedly intolerable; D'Alembert too excellent to be quite satisfactory; Condorcet almost sentimental and pedantic enough to explain his hideous fate. If we would seek a rival in charm to Diderot, we shall find him not among the men of letters but in the statesman of the Encyclopædists, the proud, the simple, the blameless Turgot.

Of all the great French writers of the eighteenth century, Diderot has the smallest reputation as a pure artist. Lord Morley, in his standard biography, has tacitly subscribed to the prevailing opinion by calling his book *Diderot and the Encyclopædists*. But noble as the *Encyclopædia* was, it is time to pull out Diderot from where he lies crushed beneath its ruins. For the *Encyclopædia* was in truth to our author a sublime servitude, which has stereotyped the designer's fame. It was in many ways the supreme expression of the eighteenth century, the answer of the new society to the ages of faith. His own age regarded Diderot as its artificer and future generations have echoed the applause. Diderot seems to have accepted this judgment on himself. No man was ever freer from the vanity of authorship. He tossed off his writings and then tossed them into the corner as though they were mere rubbish, "*ces petits cahiers, qui sont de petits chefs-d'œuvre*," as Sainte-Beuve said of them. His masterpiece in dialogue and narrative, *Le Neveu de Rameau*, first faced the public favour in 1805, and then in a German translation by Goethe. The manuscript was picked up on the quais in the '90's of last century. *La Religieuse* was published in 1796, the *Rêve de D'Alembert* not till 1830. His contemporaries, could not then judge fairly of his powers as a creative artist. To them he was known mostly, apart from his work on the *Encyclopædia*, for his *Lettre sur les aveugles*, which got him into prison, and his unsatisfactory novel *Les bijoux indiscrets*; his dreary wastes of art criticism, his *Lettre sur les sourds et muets*, a brilliant contribution to the art of pantomime, and his unsuccessful attempts in play-writing in which, however, he inaugurated for good or for bad the realistic play.

Rémy de Gourmont has objected to Diderot that he had no style. If this were the whole truth, there would be an end of Diderot. If a man has no style, we have no use for him; he can stretch out his bed in histories of literature : and be allowed to slumber there. But naturally it is not the whole truth. Diderot suffers certainly from having neither the classical beauty of Voltaire nor the romantic beauty of Rousseau. He is often hasty, muddy, careless. For all the eighteen volumes, which so exasperated Carlyle, whose own *œuvre* was, however, even more voluminous, he sometimes seems an amateur of letters or rather, perhaps, a mere journalist, without the something that is always added to the journalism of Voltaire. But one stylistic quality he had in its extremest form, that of getting his soul down onto paper. We always hear the conversationalist across the writer. When he paid his famous visit to Great Catherine, he gave her advice, which she thought rather unnecessary, on every detail of her already perfect system of Government. But worse than this impertinence was his habit of driving home his points by pinching the plump Imperial knee. Eventually the Empress put a table between herself and him. It is with his writings as with his conversation: he pinches our knee with every sentence. But, our knees not being Imperial, we encourage rather than reject the familiarity. He is so anxious to make us sensible that he has no time to waste: he can hardly finish an argument before a new one, even better, has loomed on the horizon. So on he rushes, like the tide, without time for correction or reflection, often confused, unconvincing, incomplete, but rarely, when once he has got going, boring or bored. Eventually we are carried away by our perorator's enthusiasm and adopt his views to give him pleasure. The merits of Diderot the writer are, then, swiftness, wit, pugnacity, enthusiasm, the qualities of Diderot the man. But those who like everything to remind them of something else, the contented men of this world, the high spirited rats ever gnawing at the cheese of information, the pedants who have alone found out the elixir of happiness, cannot but find interesting such a passage as this, which occurs towards the end of the second part of the *Supplement to the Voyage of Bougainville*.

"Eloigne-toi à moins que tes yeux cruels ne se plaisent à des spectacles de mort : éloigne-toi, va, et puissent les mers coupables qui t'ont epargné dans ton voyage, s'absoudre et nous venger en t'engloutissant avant ton retour ! Et vous, Tahitiens, rentrez dans vos cabanes, rentrez tous : et que ces indignes étrangers n'entendent à leur départ que le flot qui mugit et ne voient que l'écume dont sa fureur blanchit une rive deserte.

"A peine eût-il achevé que la foule des habitants disparut : un vaste silence régna dans toute l'étendue de l'île : et l'un entendit que le sifflement aigu des vents et le bruit sourd des eaux sur toute la longeur de la côte : on eût dit que l'air et la mer, sensibles à la voix du vieillard, se disposaient à lui obéir."

Here we have not only the epithets and the atmosphere but something of the measure of Chateaubriand. Diderot was half-way to the romantic movement.

Much has been written, by persons far more competent than the translator, of Diderot's philosophical and scientific opinions. An adequate exegesis is to be found in every intelligent treatise on eighteenth-century thought. Diderot was not fully equipped to be a professional philosopher. He was rather a propagandist for other people's opinions or what he would have probably preferred to call *les lumières*. His opinions frequently changed and were frequently obscure. In philosophy, as in writing, he was something of an amateur and had not thought everything out.

The present series of translations is intended rather to give pleasure than to trace the growth of the author's mind and to demarcate the exact limits of his scepticism. Nevertheless, the reader unacquainted with Diderot's writings may carry away with him, if he cares to read this volume, some idea of Diderot's general attitude towards life. Perhaps it may be roughly summarized as follows:

"It is exciting to be a materialist. The more I can bar out any but material agencies in the construction of the Universe, the better I shall be pleased. Mysticism is tedious, commonsense romantic. To trace the development of D'Alembert from the earth-mould to mathematics is to me worth all the religions of the world. But materialism I believe to be not only pleasant but true. We know very little science as yet, but the more we know, the more we shall explain. Why D'Alembert is different from a cow, I cannot quite understand. But some day science will explain.

"Never forget the respect due to your neighbour. Man is a free, thinking, feeling being, whom you have no right to persecute, still less to own. Perhaps science will one day enable us to get along without servants. I dislike most religious people because they do not wish me to think, feel, and be free. They want to mould me, to fit me into their desires and if they could they would burn me at the stake. Any amount of nonsense came into the world with religion, particularly the idea of sin. It is our business on earth to be happy. We must test everything from the new outlook of private good and public utility. This is the law of nature: and all other laws, civil or religious, are nonsense. Stop persecuting people and you will find that most of them will become quite amiable. Remorse and the fear of punishment are the great breeders of criminals. The tyranny of the priest and the monarch is written all over the history of the world. Religious enthusiasm drives men mad with hatred and can do no good to morals. Do not put too much strain on human frailty. Be compassionate. Let your heart go out to the oppressed, be they women, savages, or animals. Think the best of everybody and thus you will raise them to your own level.

"The Christian God, as developed by theologians, is a fiend. Still, if the idea of God makes you good and happy I do not wish to intervene. Clear your mind of dogma. Conduct is of far more importance than metaphysics.

"I have enjoyed all sorts of things in life: books, women, pictures, friends, controversy, science, and toasting my toes before the fire. These are the things that count. Do not add to the unnecessary work of the world by inventing large numbers of improvements. Unfortunately it is so difficult to know where to stop.

"Do not be a fanatic and spend your time putting your head into nooses. Do not break the law if you can help it, though you should clamour incessantly for reform. Warm feelings and commonsense make the world go round.

"There is no reason to believe in any after-life. So you might as well face the fact at once. If God is at once omnipotent and benevolent, why is there so much misery in the world? Avoid prejudice, and criticize everything on principle. Do not believe a thing to be true merely because Aristotle said it was so. An idea is all the better for being a new one."

Such is the general work-a-day philosophy of Diderot, who was a compound of commonsense and sentimentality. Philosophers will find more than this in his writings, and will be glad to prove where Diderot followed Descartes, and where he misunderstood Leibnitz or how far he cribbed everything from Condillac and D'Alembert. But for a change, the translator would be glad if his readers regarded the following pieces mainly as works of art. That may perhaps be arrogance in him, as it is not difficult to render an author's thought: it is harder to capture something of his charm. Nevertheless, the translator hopes that enough will survive of the original to indicate wherein lies the author's strength.

Most of the pieces that follow are in form dramatic. We should not seek overmuch to find in the opinions expressed the thought of the author. In the longest individual dialogue translated, a conversation in three acts with four characters—Diderot, D'Alembert, Julie de Lespinasse, and Doctor Bordeu—we see most of the philosophical opinions of the author. The science is naturally entirely out of date, and consequently the philosophy based upon it. The form, however, is as fresh as may be. The characters are living and distinct. Diderot is what he was in life, enthusiastic, omniscient, tireless, impatient of contradiction. In the first act he wears D'Alembert out with his unceasing flow of speech; D'Alembert is not anxious to continue the conversation. He wishes merely to go to bed. He will almost give up his belief in God in order to be allowed a moment's peace. But however much he assents to one paradox, his friend immediately presses him into another. Diderot will not allow D'Alembert even to be a sceptic. D'Alembert goes home at length, but not to sleep.

In Act II D'Alembert has passed a disturbed night. He is haunted by the nightmare of his evening's conversation. Julie de Lespinasse takes down his ravings, and calls for Doctor Bordeu to see the patient. When the Doctor arrives, Julie is alone visible, but D'Alembert is half-asleep half-awake behind a curtain, and occasionally contributes to the conversation. Julie begins by reading to the Doctor the ravings of her friend, but he is able to persuade her that these supposed ravings are in truth fragments of a highly interesting discussion on the nature of matter. Julie is a foil to the argument. She does not think she has a speculative mind, and continually falls into a fallacy. But she is extremely quick-witted, and her contributions to the discussion always help matters on. Time flies by as the two, occasionally assisted by D'Alembert, build up a theory of matter. The Doctor is always trying to go away, but he cannot do so. The charm of Julie's conversation is too great. He misses an appointment, but admits that his treatment would probably be useless. At twelve o'clock he has to go, but agrees to try and come back at two to lunch and a continuation of the discussion. A short third act in the form of a tête-à-tête between Julie and the Doctor finishes off the play, D'Alembert having gone out to pay a call. In this third act the Doctor pushes the 'scientific' and materialistic view of conduct to its extreme point and uses arguments, which Diderot has himself combated in other of his writings. The Doctor is artistically a charming figure, and serves an artistic purpose in the dialogue. He is not always to be taken as the spokesman of Diderot's thoughts. This dialogue in three parts was composed in 1769, and Diderot was thoroughly delighted with it. "The maddest and deepest thing ever written," he wrote to Sophie Voland; "there are five or six pages that will make your sister's hair stand on end." This three-act conversation was read aloud to his friends, and in this case Diderot could not willingly resign himself to not publishing what he rightly considered a masterpiece. Julie de Lespinasse, however, did not take the same view of the matter. There were some remarks on the peculiar nature of her relations with D'Alembert which she might well have disliked being printed. Hence she requested Diderot to burn the manuscript, and he did what she asked. Without Diderot's knowledge, however, extra copies had been made by friends to whom the dialogues had been shown, and in 1830 they were eventually made public to the delight of posterity without any failure of honour on the part of Diderot.

Certainly in these three dialogues Diderot, speaking through the mouths of various speakers, has roughly stated his views on matter as they appeared to him at the moment of writing. He does not succeed in making himself clear and, in his desire to explain everything, he runs far ahead of his comprehension of nature. But, artistically, the form of the thing is wellnigh perfect. English readers, like Sophie Voland's sister, may object to the coarseness of certain pages. Diderot was not, if you will, an excessively delicate-minded man, but the 'objectionable" passages are not there for indecency's sake. Rather Diderot, in his reaction against Ecclesiastical Ethics, came to find something beautiful in the stark processes of nature. He would write the poetry of physiology. If the translator has had any success with his versions the reader will observe the style becoming heightened, as the subject becomes materialistic or even physical. For Diderot showers upon the body the sentiments other people reserve for the soul. It is easy to think such an attitude, in its way, another form of sentimentality, mistaken, uninteresting, or silly. But any reader must try to comprehend it or he will fail to see the point of Diderot either as a thinker or as an artist. It is excusable to be offended by Diderot, absurd to be shocked by him. For he was always bent on making impure things pure, the converse of the attitude adopted by the salacious writer. Nor must we overlook the devices by which the author, with great artistic skill, puts a stopper on the argument, when he feels it growing too coarse for art.

The Supplement to the Voyage of Bougainville was written in 1772 and appeared in 1796, thus being yet another of Diderot's posthumously published works.

Bougainville, the first Frenchman to circumnavigate the globe, accomplished his task in 1766–1769. The narrative of his journey appeared in 1771, and Diderot's *Supplement* is a philosophical comment upon it. At first sight this *Supplement* appears to occupy a sensational place in the history of the Noble Savage, whose career eighteenth-century fancy coloured in its most seductive light. It is agreeable to say that Diderot was the inventor of the Noble Savage and thus help to take the wind out of Rousseau's sails. As a matter of fact, the Noble Savage was a sturdy stripling by the time Diderot met him; Mrs Aphra Behn might claim to have been one of his midwives. Further, it hardly appears that this attractive personage played a large part in Diderot's emotional life. We know from his correspondence with Sophie Voland that he thought but poorly of the Chinese frenzy that was raging among his acquaintance at the same date, and in his dissertation *On Women* he paints a very different picture of savage life. The *Supplement to the Voyage of Bougainville* cannot well be even regarded as a serious *Utopia* like Sir Thomas More's or like Plato's *Republic* or the dreams of Montaigne in his essay *On Cannibals*. Diderot, in truth, hardly even pretends that he wishes us to take his *mise-en-scène* seriously. He gives away his position on the last page, in which he earnestly urges his readers not for an instant to behave as though they were already in Tahiti. His reason in choosing the form he did for his dialogue was artistic. He wanted to say a number of very offensive things about French civilization, and he saw that he could say what he wanted in its extremist form by putting his sentiments into the mouth of a noble savage. He also perceived that by so doing he could the better exasperate a number of people whom he heartily disliked. It may be said that his main motive in writing *Bougainville* was a motive still happily potent in the human heart—the desire to annoy. In *Bougainville* the rhetorical gifts of the author reach a very high level. There is in the writing a beauty and a pathos rare with Diderot. He did not believe an instant in his venerable old primitive, but he has made of him a fine old fellow, a trifle melodramatic perhaps, European, and (as he laughingly admits) in fact Parisian, and extremely *bon ton* in his expressions and ideas—still an impressive creation. There is a genuine charm about the descriptions of village feasting and rustic melody which live in the memory of the reader. Further, Diderot shows a very sensitive artistry in his presentation of the Chaplain, the hero, or the victim, if you will, of the whole escapade. He is an intelligent, broad-minded, civilized, and conscientious man, who slips from the path of rectitude only after almost intolerable provocation. A gin-sodden, brutal missionary would have in any case been an artistic atrocity, but it may be permissible to find in this kindly, if humorous, sketch some gracious memory of the admirable education Diderot himself received from the Jesuits, in whose school he was so happy: the Jesuits who, unluckily for themselves, trained so adequately the brilliant intellects that were to pursue them to their doom.

The three pieces that follow need but few introductory remarks, being simply *les petits cahiers, qui sont de petits chef-d'œuvres*. *Regrets on an Old Dressing-gown* was published in 1772. Its charm cannot escape the most casual reader. From the point of view of Diderot's general writings, the chief thing to note is, perhaps, the fact that it affords us a glimpse of the author's Art-criticism, which occupies such a disproportionate space in his writings. He was one of the first real art-critics in the modern sense of the word, one of those unfortunates who trail round exhibitions and then endeavour to embroider on their emotions.

Diderot spent an immense amount of time in this way. He was particularly suited for his rôle by the fact that he quite obviously had no genuine æsthetic reaction whatever to visual art. He liked a picture that told a story, preferably a sentimental one, and was at his happiest weeping over Greuze's canary. Like other critics, he tried to get as quickly as possible off the subject and to write about something else, but unlike most other art critics he often contrived to write charmingly. He was, in any case, hopelessly handicapped by his limited knowledge of the subject. He had seen very little Italian painting, had no genuine standard of values, and hence very little sense of proportion. He was, in fact, like the young Mexican in his famous parable, afloat on the ocean without chart or rudder. Many persons, however, will find literary charm, if no æsthetic criticism of value, in his endless series *Les Salons*.

On Women, which appeared in 1772, is little more than a review on Thomas's *Dissertation on Women*, which was published in 1772. It is a passionately feministic outburst, a fascinating mixture of the out-of-date and the perennially true. Diderot was hardly interested in politics in the narrower sense of the word, and in *Sur les femmes* he shows how essentially *ancien régime* his outlook was. He could not offer to women a better estate than that of fairydom, and he was miles away from the Mary Wollstoncrafts and the Olympe de Gouges of the new generation: his ideal, at any rate, was not to triumph with Lyon's café and the typewriter. Apart from the charm of the style, it appeals to us as showing the general compassion of the author and his tremendous desire that all oppression should be remedied. The passage about native life on the banks of the Orinoco should be read in connection with the *Supplement to the Voyage of Bougainville*, if we wish to form an estimate of Diderot's views on civilization. It would probably be not far from the truth to say that he disliked rusticity and urbanity with equal violence.

The *Conversation with the Maréchale de . . .*, one of the most charming of his writings, need not detain us long. It is supposed to be an idealized version of a real conversation with the Maréchale de Broglie, and was published in 1777, almost as soon as written. This dialogue is notable for "the parable of the young Mexican," which, owing to its rare beauty, has been quite gratuitously attributed to Rousseau. The beauty of its literary form perhaps recalls Rousseau, but in its general amiability and optimism it is Diderot through and through. The *Conversation with the Maréchale*, in its protest against persecution and the instinct for futile self-sacrifice, probably represents as well as anything else Diderot's general attitude towards life.

II

This is no place for a life of Diderot, though a new biography supplementary to, and critical of, Lord Morley's standard work would be a welcome addition to modern literature. Still, a few biographical details will hardly be out of place. Diderot was born at Langres on the 5th of October, 1713. His father was a successful and highly intelligent cutler, a master worker, and an inventor. The warm-hearted sentimental Denis, an enthusiastic supporter of family-life for other people, subsequently wove a romance round his straightforward, hard-headed father, though the two were never destined to live together in amity. We may deduce that his father was a respectable, obstinate, though intellectual, old man, who disliked nonsense in young people, and thought they ought to settle down early and become useful members of society. The easy-going, over-talkative, extravagant, excessively generous, feckless Denis must have seemed to him a poor return for a life of honourable thrift. Fortunately, old Madame Diderot, like Madame la Maréchale in the dialogue, was made of softer stuff, and was always sending something out of her savings to assist her young scapegrace in Paris. Yet his early years meant much to Diderot. When he was editing the *Encyclopædia*, he was always inside workshops, documenting himself about the details of industry, and delighting the workmen with his quickness and enthusiasm. His childhood's acquaintance with the inside of a workshop had come in useful. There was nothing of the aristocrat about Denis. Early he was put to school with the Jesuits, and his enthusiastic imagination was quickly fired by his teachers. He saw himself a missionary. But his father, *un parfait honnête homme*, quickly nipped this in the bud, and Diderot was sent up to Paris, to attend the Collège d'Harcourt. His terms completed, various reputable openings were offered and all refused. The cutler lost his temper, and poor Denis, who could do nothing but talk, was left upon the streets. His position was, officially, desperate in the extreme. But we may hazard the belief that in the Café de la Régence, where he hobnobbed with the neveu de Rameau and other unworthies, he picked up a good many free meals. For he was a tireless talker, and the world, on the whole, is kind to chatterboxes. Anyhow, he got through the day somehow, reading, giving lessons, talking, and above all gaining that general knowledge of humanity in which he surpasses all his contemporaries. Then he fell ill, and was nursed by a sympathetic young idiot Toinette Champion, to whom he proposed, during convalescence, and by whom he was, needless to say, accepted. This was the final blow to the sensible old cutler, and, when the young hopeful went back to Langres to solicit the family blessing and an allowance, he was turned out of the house. So back he went to Paris, as penniless as ever without having written a line, to marry his Toinette off-hand.

The cutler had been perfectly right. The marriage was a catastrophe, the only fruit of which was the daughter he loved so well, and who was to be his first biographer. So he looked round for a mistress, and found one in Madame de Puysieux, an odious woman, who, unlike Toinette, needed to be amused, and the necessity of raising money to amuse her caused Denis to commence author. *Les bijoux indiscrets* we owe to this liaison and *Essai sur les aveugles*, which got the author into Vincennes, an experience he greatly disliked despite the kindness of the Governor, M. du Châtelet, the husband of Voltaire's Semiramis. One evening he got out of prison and obtained visual proof of the infidelity of Madame de Puysieux, who had excusably thought everything safe during her lover's incarceration. *L'Essai sur les aveugles* is a charming book, but perhaps its chief importance lies in the fact that its publication brought him into touch with the leading literary men of the day, especially Voltaire, who writes to him in a spirit half-congratulatory, half-critical. "But I am not of Saunderson's* opinion, who denies the existence of God, because he is born blind. I may be mistaken, but in my place I should have recognized the existence of a very intelligent being, who had given me so many compensations for my sight." Diderot's answer is significant. "The opinions of Saunderson are no more mine than yours. But this may be because I am not blind." This is a very characteristic observation, which may be commended to all over-anxious to draw up a cut-and-dried scheme of Diderot's opinions. Diderot, at any rate,

* A blind Cambridge Don, the 'hero' of the Essay.

in the latter part of his life, was certainly an atheist, but he was far from being an opinionated one. One might almost say that Saunderson's point of view pleased him æsthetically and that, hence, he wrote it down with enthusiasm. He did not, therefore, either believe or disbelieve it. He was often more pleased with the processes than the conclusions of the human mind. In 1745 Diderot began to busy himself, first in collaboration with D'Alembert, with the preparation of the *Encyclopædia*, an undertaking which was to fill the next twenty years of his life, a crushing work rendered more crushing by the dangers to which the editor was regularly exposed from the operations of the royal censor. Financially it was rendered possible by the generosity of Madame Geoffrin, politically by the fitful patronage of Madame de Pompadour and the secret encouragement of the chief of police. Now-a-days we may say that any great danger to the *Encyclopædia* was more apparent than real. But it can hardly have appeared such to the harassed, harrowed, over-hurried Diderot. The *Encyclopædia* was an ungrateful task, but at least it made Diderot a European figure, a symbol of enlightenment and exact knowledge. Anyone who wished to be thought at all clever, either in France or abroad, had to be a supporter of the *Encyclopædia*. All famous people wanted to write for the *Encyclopædia*. And many other people who were not famous at all. A lady living in the country sent up an article on the petticoat, saying that, if her article was accepted, she could provide a number more in the same style. The article was accepted. So the crushing labour went on, wearing out Diderot's health and ruining his never flourishing finances. Great Catherine, as the Queen of European intelligence, bought his library and installed him in it as librarian on a salary, an action for which she should have credit with posterity. The books were taken to Russia after Diderot's death, and are at present in the Hermitage. His chief consolations were his daughter and his friend Sophie Voland, with whom, after several disappointments due to his impulsive temperament, he at length found lasting happiness. His large correspondence with her proves a thousand times over the beauty and comfort of the relationship, and it is difficult to see why critics, including Lord Morley, have found it necessary to throw doubt upon her charms. Until her death, a few months before his, she made Diderot completely happy. While busy on the *Encyclopædia* Diderot was also busy in other ways. His play *Le fils naturel* appeared in 1757, *Le père de famille* in 1758. Frankly they are intolerable reading (*Est il bon, est il mauvais?* is more amusing than the others), but at the same time they are original. Before then there were tragedies in verse and comedies in prose. Diderot invented 'domestic' tragedy, 'naturalistic' tragedy, the 'génre sérieux,' the 'génre ennuyeux'—call it what you will. We hardly feel grateful to him for his wonderful invention.

In 1773 Diderot set out via Holland to visit Great Catherine and thank her personally for her tremendous kindness. On the way he composed *Jacques le Fataliste*, one of his most remarkable works, which was not published till 1792. The visit was hardly a success. His friend Falconet made himself extremely disagreeable, and Diderot was not sufficiently flexible to be a good courtier. Diderot and Catherine probably parted with mutual satisfaction. He returned home changed and aged, but as gay, amusing, and good-natured as ever. By now he was a leading figure in Paris and welcome everywhere, a brilliant conversationalist or a tireless chatterbox, whichever you may prefer to call it. He was particularly the friend of Grimm, Madame Geoffrin, Madame D'Epinay, and the Baron d'Holbach, with whom atheism amounted to an obsession. "The conversation of Diderot," writes the delightful 'enlightened' Abbé Morellet, "had great power and great charm: his argument was animated by perfect good faith, was subtle without being obscure, varied in form, brilliant in imagination, fruitful and stimulating in ideas. We flowed down its stream for hours together as on a clear peaceful river on each bank of which the country was finely cultivated and sprinkled with handsome houses." Ten days before his death Diderot moved into a fine new house in the Rue Richelieu, which again he owed to the good nature of Catherine, whose conduct is all the more to be commended as she had evidently found his society a disappointment. In the spring of 1784 he had had an attack, which could only mean one thing, and dropsy set in. On the evening of 30th of July he died peacefully at table, struck down by apoplexy. His wife asked him a question and, as he did not answer, she looked up and saw that he was dead. He had died as he had hoped, in full possession of his faculties; God, like Great Catherine, had not the heart to punish him too severely for his impertinences.

Diderot's was externally an uneventful, routinish life. Once he knew prison, and frankly, never had the intention of returning there. He suffered not at all from that inferiority complex which continually drove on Voltaire and Rousseau to further and further indiscretions. Diderot's life was given up to hard work and hard talk. He was essentially a good man. When a blackmailer waited on him with a libel and endeavoured to extort money, Diderot contented himself with improving the style of the document and sending the wretch away to get what money he could for it. The stories of his good nature are endless. He would always share his last halfpenny with anyone, and the fact that he was so genuinely amiable made other people amiable in return. Rousseau is, except his father, the only man with whom he succeeded in quarrelling, and Rousseau could quarrel with anyone. This absence of quarrelling comes as a great relief in the life of Diderot. It sets him as a man above and apart from his contemporaries. He has become with Voltaire and Rousseau the third person in the trinity that upset the *ancien régime*. We may venture to think that nothing was further from his thoughts. Voltaire, all through his political campaigns, dreamed of himself as first minister to a benevolent despot introducing reforms with a magic wand amid the adoration of a contented and virtuous peasantry. Rousseau was driven on by a profound misanthropy to desire the destruction of the existing order. Diderot was less self-seeking than either of these two. At bottom an unopinionated man, he was particularly unopinionated about politics. In the *Encyclopædia* he reflects the general opinion of society about such well-recognized abuses as the *taille* or the *gabelle*. But, in truth, he was not a politician at all. He cared above all for intellectual freedom. "Give people a chance and they will not persecute. They can be left to go free their own way and we can go on discussing the nature of matter." Such was the burden of his faith. It was easy to see why Voltaire was the hero of the first revolutionaries and Rousseau of the Jacobins. Neither party was over-anxious to offer homage to Diderot. Yet they might with justice have done so: for through the *Encyclopædia* Diderot became the spokesman of unbelief and materialism, that necessary background for the *honnête homme* who first precipitated the Revolution, and finally, after some anxious moments, went off with the profits. This eventuality, had Diderot been able to foresee it, he would have heartily disliked ; for there was nothing whatever of the *bourgeois* about him. He was an adventurous, quixotic, reckless spirit, and this is what makes his moderation so admirable. His enthusiasm and his commonsense were continually reacting on each other. He was sentimental to the core, but beside Voltaire, beside Rousseau, beside Condorcet he was essentially an unromantic character. The good sense of the provincial cutler clings about him to the end. Despite his whimsical Utopias, like Tahiti, he wove no huge schemes for social and moral regeneration. Doubtless he thought that mere irreligion would do more good than has actually been the case; but in general he was content to combat superstition when he met it, and meanwhile he would always lend anybody five shillings. His whole private and public life was spent trying to do private and public good, and so he retained his sweetness through the hard years spent with the neveu de Rameau or in toil, agitation, and poverty when engaged on the *Encyclopædia*. His faults spring from excessive sanity. Nearly all intelligent people suffer from inhibitions, which prevent their enjoying the frank outspokenness of the average sensual man. Hence they are offended by Diderot's absence of over-sensibility. Sainte-Beuve in a brilliant, unfavourable essay has collected all the examples of bad taste he can find in Diderot. He repeats with particular disapproval the account Diderot gives of how as a young man he used to go into a bookshop where the pretty young Mademoiselle Babuti, soon to become the wife and the scourge of Greuze, served behind the counter. He used to enjoy asking her for a number of slightly indecent works and observing the looks of assumed embarrassment which brought a blush to the cheeks of the pretty flirt. The offence is presumably less in the action than in the fact that the offender thought fit to mention it again without remorse. As an art critic presumably hard up for copy, he became distinctly irrelevant about the young landscape painter Loutherbourg.

"Courage, young man, thou hast gone further than is permissible at thine age. . . . Thou hast a charming companion who will fix thee. Only leave thy workshop to consult nature. Live in the fields with thy companion, see the sun rise and set. . . . Leave your bed early, despite the charming young woman who lies beside thee."

Such unfortunate little outbursts as these have brought down on the good-natured, happy-go-lucky, improvident Diderot the rage of the mandarins of literature, Sainte-Beuve, Lord Morley, Carlyle, and it is certainly unfortunate for the eighteenth century that so far the nineteenth century has been its only critic. At the same time, it would be absurd to say that the attitude of Diderot to physical things was not one of great importance to himself and should be of equal importance in our estimate of him. If you will, there was in him a grain of coarseness, though that is not quite the word. But there was something peasant-like, something plebeian about Diderot, and in this he is a typical Frenchman. For nearly all Frenchmen are peasants two generations back. Nevertheless, it is more respectful to admit the existence of this quality, whatever it may be, than either to overlook it or to abuse him for something else. Nobody who had read his life or writings with any care could assert that he was anything but a virtuous man. He was essentially a member of the intellectual middle-class in the eighteenth century, and one in whom ordinary human qualities were developed to the highest point. Nobody was ever less afflicted by the eccentricity of genius or by those irritating qualities attendant on the artistic temperament. Where Diderot was so much we may admit without blushing that he lacked something of the sensibility of a poet.

III

For help in the preparation of these versions, I wish particularly to thank Professor Charles Singer for assistance in the elucidation of some medical terms in *D'Alembert's Dream* and to Mr R. S. Partridge for his frenzies of inspiration when confronted with some almost unintelligible passages. *D'Alembert's Dream* is an extremely difficult piece of French. I hope there are no longer any gross errors in my version. Readers may rest assured that any inaccuracies that still linger are not there owing to absence of pains on my part.

I owe a particular debt to my friend, Mr R. F. Wright, who could hardly have taken more interest in the preparation of this volume had his own personal honour been involved. Every page has benefited by his help. Naturally he is in no way responsible for any errors remaining in the versions.

FRANCIS BIRRELL.

CONVERSATION BETWEEN D'ALEMBERT AND DIDEROT

D'Alembert: I grant it is difficult to accept the existence of a Being so contradictory in nature: a Being which exists everywhere and relates to no particular point in space; a Being which is without space and yet occupies space: which is quite complete in each part of this space: which differs essentially from nature and yet is united to it: which follows and removes matter, while itself remaining motionless; a Being, of which I have not the slightest conception. Yet quite other difficulties lie in wait for the man who rejects this Being. Take this Feeling, which you substitute for it. If it be a general and essential quality of matter, it follows that a stone must feel.

Diderot: And why not?

D'Alembert: I find it hard to believe.

Diderot: Yes, because a man cuts, carves, and crushes the stone and does not hear it scream.

D'Alembert: I should like you to tell me what distinction you make between man and statue, flesh and marble.

Diderot: Not very much. Marble is made with flesh and flesh with marble.

D'Alembert: Still one is not the other.

Diderot: Just as what you call live force is not dead force.

D'Alembert: I don't follow.

Diderot: Let me explain. The transplanting of a body from one place to another is not movement, only effect. Movement resides equally in the body whether it be transplanted or motionless.

D'Alembert: That is a new way of looking at it.

Diderot: And none the less true for that. Remove the obstacle which prevents the transplanting from one place to another of this motionless body and it will be transplanted. Suppress by a rapid rarefication the air which surrounds this enormous trunk of oak and the water it contains will disperse it in a hundred thousand fragments. I say just the same of your own body.

D'Alembert: Very well. But what is the relation between movement and feeling? Could it be that you recognized an active feeling and a passive feeling in the same way as there is a live force and a dead force, which manifests itself by pressure: an active feeling which is characterized by a certain remarkable behaviour in animals and perhaps in plants: and a passive feeling, which one can test by its passage to an active state of feeling?

Diderot: Exactly. You have put it perfectly.

D'Alembert: Then the statue has only passive feeling, while men, animals, and perhaps even plants are endowed with active feeling.

Diderot: That no doubt is one difference between the block of marble and the flesh tissue. But you certainly understand that it is not the only one.

D'Alembert: Most assuredly. Whatever resemblance there may be between the external form of man and statue, there is no point of contact between their internal organisms. The chisel of the most cunning sculptor does not create even an epidermis. There is a very simple process by which the passage from the state of live force to that of dead force can be effected. It is an experiment which is repeated under our eyes a hundred times a day. On the other hand, I do not see how to make a body pass from the state of passive to that of active feeling.

DIDEROT: Only because you do not wish to. It is quite a common phenomenon.

D'ALEMBERT: And this quite common phenomenon, what is it, if you please?

DIDEROT: I am going to tell you, since you choose to be shy about it. It occurs every time you eat.

D'ALEMBERT: Every time I eat!

DIDEROT: Yes, for what do you do when you eat? You remove the obstacles which prevented what you are eating being able to feel. You assimilate it with yourself. You make flesh of it. You animalize it. You give it feeling. And what you do to a piece of food, I shall do, when I please, to marble.

D'ALEMBERT: And how?

DIDEROT: I shall make it eatable.

D'ALEMBERT: Make marble eatable! I don't think that can be easy.

DIDEROT: It is only my business to indicate the process to you. I take that statue, you see there. I put it in a mortar, and with great blows from a pestle . . .

D'ALEMBERT: Gently there. It's Falconet's* masterpiece. Now if it were something by Huez or a man like him——

DIDEROT: Falconet won't mind. The statue is paid for, and Falconet cares little for present, nothing for future fame.

D'ALEMBERT: Go on then. Grind it to powder.

DIDEROT: When the block of marble is reduced to impalpable powder, I mix this powder with *humus*,

* Falconet (1716–1791), a sculptor greatly admired in Europe and a client of Catherine the Great. Translated Pliny's writings on art. He professed a heroic contempt for fame.

or leaf-mould. I compound them well together. I water the mixture. I allow it to rot one year, two years, a century. Time matters nothing to me. When everything has been transformed into a more or less homogeneous piece of matter, *humus*, do you know what I shall do with it?

D'Alembert: I am sure you never eat *humus*.

Diderot: No. But there is a method by which I can unite with myself, can appropriate the *humus*, a *latus*, as the chemists say.

D'Alembert: And this *latus* is a plant?

Diderot: Exactly. I sow peas, beans, cabbages, and other leguminous plants. The plants are fed by the earth and I feed myself with the plants.

D'Alembert: Whether it be true or false, I like this passage from marble to *humus*, from *humus* to the vegetable kingdom, from the vegetable to the animal kingdom, to flesh.

Diderot: And so I consider flesh (or soul, as my daughter calls it) actively feeling matter. And if I am not solving the problem you put to me, at least I am getting near it. For you will grant that it is much further from a block of marble to a being which feels than from a being that feels to a being that thinks.

D'Alembert: Agreed. But for all that, the feeling being has not yet become the thinking being.

Diderot: Before taking a step forward, let me tell you the story of one of the greatest mathematicians in Europe. What was this marvellous being originally? Nothing.

D'Alembert: How nothing? Nothing springs from nothing.

Diderot: You take my words too literally. This is what I want to say. Before his mother, the beautiful and criminal canoness Tencin,* had reached the age of puberty, before the soldier La Touche was adolescent, the molecules which were to form the first rudiments of my mathematician were scattered in the young and delicate organisms of these two, filtered with the lymph, circulated with the blood, until they arrived at the reservoirs destined for their mingling, the testicles and ovaries of their father and mother. Now see this rare germ formed: see it, as common opinion says, brought into the womb by the Fallopian tubes: attached to the womb by a long stalk, increasing by stages and advancing to the state of fœtus. Now is the moment come for leaving its dark prison. Behold it born, and exposed on the steps of St Jean le Rond, which gave it its name: pulled out of the Foundlings, attached to the breast of the good glass-seller Madame Rousseau, weaned and grown great in mind and body, writer, engineer, mathematician. And how is this done? By eating and other purely mechanical operations. Here is the general formula in four words. Eat, digest, distil, *in vasi licito et fiat homo secundum artem.* But he who would develop before the Academy how a man or animal is progressively formed, should employ only material agencies, whose successive stages would be—a passive being, a feeling being, a thinking being, a being who resolves the Precession of the Equinoxes, a sublime being, a marvellous being, a being ageing, failing, dying, dissolved, and returned to the leaf-mould.

D'Alembert: You do not, then, believe in pre-existent germs?

Diderot: No.

D'Alembert: I am delighted to hear it.

* D'Alembert was the illegitimate son of the famous Mme de Tencin by the Chevalier la Touche. His mother exposed him at birth, as Diderot relates.

Diderot: They are contrary to experiment and reason: contrary to experiment, which would search vainly for these germs in the egg and in most animals before a certain age: contrary to reason, which tells us that the divisibility of matter has a limit in nature, though it may have none in imagination and shrinks at conceiving an elephant ready formed in an atom, and in this atom another elephant already formed, and so on indefinitely.

D'Alembert: But without these pre-existing germs, the original generation of animals is difficult to grasp.

Diderot: If the egg's priority over the hen, or the hen's over the egg troubles you, it is because you suppose that originally they were the same as they are at present. What lunacy! One no more knows what they have been than what they will become. The worm which stirs in the slime is proceeding perhaps to the estate of a huge animal. The enormous animal which terrifies us by its size is proceeding perhaps to the estate of a worm, or is perhaps a peculiar and momentary production of this planet.

D'Alembert: Quite how did you say that?

Diderot: I said . . . But that will take us too far away from our first discussion.

D'Alembert: And what does that matter? We shall come back to it or not, as the case may be.

Diderot: May I put the clock on some few thousand years?

D'Alembert: Why not? Nature does not bother about time.

Diderot: You will let me snuff out the sun.

D'Alembert: All the more readily, as it will not be the first sun to be snuffed out.

Diderot: The sun once snuffed out, what will happen? Plants will perish, animals will perish, and behold the earth solitary and silent. Relight that star and immediately you re-establish the necessary cause of infinite new generations, in the course of whose progress through the centuries, I should not like to say whether or not our present plants and animals will be reproduced.

D'Alembert: And why should these scattered elements, when they come to reunite, not yield the same results?

Diderot: Because everything is contained in nature and because that which supposes a new phenomenon or calls back a vanished moment recreates a new world.

D'Alembert: No serious thinker would deny that. But to come back to Man, since the order of things has willed his existence. You remember you left me in the passage from the feeling to the thinking being.

Diderot: I do.

D'Alembert: You would greatly oblige me by pulling me out of it. I am anxious to turn into a thinker.

Diderot: Even if I did not succeed, what would come of it against my chain of incontrovertible facts?

D'Alembert: None, unless we stopped there dead.

Diderot: And in order to go on, should we be justified in inventing an agent contradictory in its attributes, a word devoid of sense and unintelligible?

D'Alembert: Can you tell me in what consists the existence of a feeling being in so far as his relation to himself is concerned?

D'Alembert: In the consciousness of having been himself from the first moment he thought till the present.

Diderot: And on what is this consciousness founded?

D'Alembert: On the memory of his actions.

Diderot: And say he did not possess this memory?

D'Alembert: Without this memory, he would have nothing of himself, since, only being aware of his existence at the moment of receiving an impression, he would have no history of his life. His life would be an interrupted succession of unconnected sensations.*

Diderot: Very good. And what is this memory? What does it spring from?

D'Alembert: From a certain organism which gains and loses in strength and is sometimes entirely lost.

Diderot: If, then, a being who feels and also has this organism peculiar to memory connects the impression he receives, forms by this connection a history which is that of his own life and acquires consciousness of himself, he denies, he affirms, he concludes, he thinks.

D'Alembert: That seems so. Now I have only one difficulty left.

Diderot: There you're wrong. You have heaps left.

D'Alembert: But one principal one. This. It seems to me that we can think of only one thing at a time and in order to form, I do not say those enormous chains of reasoning which embrace thousands of ideas in their circuit, but only a simple proposition, there must, one would think, be two things present, the object that seems to rest under the eye of the understanding, while the understanding is busy with the quality it will allow or deny to the object.

Diderot: I think so too. And this has sometimes made me compare the fibres of our organs to sensitive

* This doctrine of 'Sensations' was common to nearly all eighteenth-century philosophers and was erected into a system by Condillac.

vibrating strings. The sensitive vibrating string oscillates and resounds long after one has plucked it. It is this oscillation, this sort of necessary resonance, which keeps the object present, while the understanding is busy on the qualities suitable to the object. But vibrating strings have another quality still, that of making other strings vibrate from them. Thus it is that a first idea calls up a second, these two a third, all three a fourth and so on, without anyone being able to put a limit to the ideas stirred up and associated in the mind of the philosopher who meditates or listens in silence and obscurity. This instrument makes astonishing jumps and an idea once stirred up can sometimes cause its corresponding harmonic to vibrate, though this harmonic is incomprehensibly far from the idea that awakened it. If this phenomenon be observable between two sounding strings which are inert and separated, how could it fail to take place between two points which are living and connected, between fibres which are continuous and feeling?

D'Alembert: That may not be true, but it is at any rate very ingenious. But I am tempted to think that you are falling imperceptibly into the error you wanted to avoid.

Diderot: Which one?

D'Alembert: You are bothered by the difference between the two substances.

Diderot: I admit it.

D'Alembert: And if you look into it closely, you are making of the philosopher's understanding a being distinct from the instrument, a sort of musician, who lends his ear to the vibrating strings and pronounces on whether they are in tune or not.

Diderot: I may have laid myself open to this objection, but still, perhaps you would not have raised it, had you considered what a difference there is between the instrument philosopher and the instrument clavecin. The instrument philsopher has feeling : he is at the same time musician and instrument. As a feeling instrument, he has immediate consciousness of the sound he is giving out. As an animal he has the memory of it. This organic faculty, by connecting up the sounds inside himself, produces and conserves the melody there. Allow the clavecin feeling and memory and tell me whether it will not repeat of itself the airs you have already played on its notes. We are instruments endowed with feeling and memory. Our senses are so many notes plucked by nature, which is all round us, and which often pluck themselves. And this, in my opinion, is all that passes in a clavecin organized like you and me. First there is an impression which has its cause inside or outside the instrument, then a sensation which springs from this impression, a sensation which lasts (for it is impossible to imagine that it is made and snuffed out in an indivisible instant): then another impression which succeeds to this sensation and which likewise has its cause inside and outside the animal, then a second sensation and voices which indicate them by natural or conventional sounds.

D'Alembert: I understand. And so, if this clavecin, which has feeling and life, were further endowed with the faculty of feeding and reproduction, it would live and breed of itself, or with the female of its species, little living resonant clavecins.

Diderot: Certainly. What else in your opinion is a chaffinch, a nightingale, a musician, or a man? What other difference do you see between a canary and a musical box?* Do you see this egg? With its aid, we can overturn all the schools of theology and all

* *Serin*, canary; *serinette*, musical box. The pun has been necessarily sacrificed in the translation.

the temples of the world. What is this egg? Before the germ is introduced, an unfeeling mass. And after the introduction of the germ, what is it still? An unfeeling mass. For this germ is itself but a passive and impercipient fluid. How will this mass pass to another state of organism? To feeling? To life? By heat. What will produce heat? Movement. What will be the successive effects of movement? Instead of answering, sit down and follow them with your eye from moment to moment. At first there is a swaying point, a thread which stretches out and takes on colour, flesh which forms: a beak, the tips of wings, eyes and claws which make their appearance: a yellow matter which winds itself round and produces intestines: it is an animal. This animal moves, stirs, cries. I hear its cries across the egg-shell. It covers itself with down: it sees. The weight of its swaying head brings its beak unceasingly against the inner wall of its prison. There, it is smashed. The animal comes out, it walks, it flies, it is provoked, it runs away, it comes up close, it complains, it suffers, it loves, it desires. It shares all your passions, goes through all your actions. Will you assert with Descartes that this is a purely imitative mechanism? Why, small children will laugh at you and philosophers will reply that if that be a mechanism, then you are such another. If you grant that between you and an animal there is no difference but one of organism, you will show sense and reason. You will be honest. But men will conclude against you that feeling, life, memory, consciousness, passions, thought can all be produced, from passive matter disposed in a certain way and impregnated with some other matter, with warmth and movement. You have only one of these two sides to choose between. You can imagine in the passive mass of the egg a hidden element, which is awaiting the egg's development to manifest its presence, or you may suppose that this imperceptible element has insinuated itself into the egg across the egg-shell, at a determined instant in its development. But what is this element? Did it occupy space or not? How has it come or escaped without moving? Where was it? What was it doing there or anywhere else? Was it in existence before? Was it expecting a home? If homogeneous, it consists of matter. If heterogeneous we can conceive neither its passivity before development, nor its activity in the developed animal.

Listen and you will be sorry for yourself. You will perceive that in order not to admit a simple supposition that explains everything, feeling, general property of matter, or product of organism, you renounce common-sense and precipitate yourself into an abyss of mysteries, contradictions, and absurdities.

D'Alembert: A supposition indeed! You are pleased to call it so. But suppose it were a quality essentially incompatible with matter?

Diderot: And how do you know that feeling is essentially incompatible with matter, you who do not know the essence of anything, neither of matter nor of feeling? Do you understand any better the nature of movement, its existence in a body and its communication from one body to another?

D'Alembert: Without grasping the nature of feeling or that of matter, I see that feeling is a simple quality, one and indivisible and incompatible with a divisible subject or agent.

Diderot: Metaphysico-theological twaddle! Surely you see that all the qualities, all the feeling forms in which matter is reclothed, are essentially individual. There is neither greater impenetrability, nor less. There is half a round body: there is not half the roundness. A body may have more or less movement. There is not more movement or less. There is no more the half or the third or the quarter of a head or an ear or a finger than the half or the third or the quarter of a thought. If in the universe there be not one molecule which resembles another, in a molecule not one point which resembles another point, you will have to agree that even the atom is endowed with a quality of its own, with an individual form: you will have to agree that division is incompatible with the essence of forms, since it destroys forms. Be a physicist and agree that an effect is produced when you see it produced, though, may be, you cannot explain the connection of cause and effect. Be a logician and do not substitute for a cause which exists and explains everything a cause which cannot be grasped, of which the connection with effect is less comprehensible still, which breeds an infinite multitude of difficulties and clears up none.

D'Alembert: But suppose I give up this cause?

Diderot: There is not more than one substance in the universe, in man, in animals. A musical box is made of wood, man of flesh. A canary is made of flesh and a musician of differently organized flesh. But the one and the other have a same origin, a same formation, the same functions, and the same end.

D'Alembert: And how is the convention of sounds between your two clavecins established?

Diderot: An animal being a feeling instrument exactly like any other, of the same conformation, built up with the same strings, plucked in the same manner by joy, sorrow, hunger, thirst, colic, admiration, terror, it cannot, whether at the Pole or under the Line, give forth different sounds. Also you find almost exactly the same interjections in all living and dead languages. We must trace to need and proximity the origin of conventional sounds. The feeling instrument or animal discovered that by giving forth such and such a sound it produced an effect on others than itself, that other feeling instruments like itself, that is to say, other similar animals, drew near, made off, asked, offered, wounded, caressed, and these effects are linked in the memory of the animal and others like itself with the formation of these sounds; and note that human relationships are built up entirely of sounds and actions. And to give my system all its force, take note again that it is subject to the same unsurmountable difficulty that Berkeley urged against the existence of bodies. There is a moment of madness to be noted when the clavecin thought it was the only clavecin in the world, and that all the harmony of the universe was contained within itself.

D'Alembert: There are many observations to be made about that.

Diderot: True.

D'Alembert: Take an example. It is not easy to grasp from your system how we form syllogisms and deduce consequences.

Diderot: That's it. We don't. They are all deduced by nature. We do no more than propound associated phenomena of which the connection is associated or contingent, phenomena which are known to us by experience—inevitable in mathematics, physics, and other exact sciences, contingent in morals, politics, and other conjectural sciences.

D'Alembert: Then the connection of phenomena is not so necessary in one case as in the other?

Diderot: That is not so. But the cause undergoes too many vicissitudes which escape us for us to be able to count infallibly on the effect that will follow. Our certainty that a violent-tempered man will lose his temper when insulted is not of the same order of certainty as that a large stone, by hitting a smaller one, will set it in motion.

D'Alembert: And your analogy?

Diderot: The analogy in the most compound cases is only a rule of three, which is exercised in the feeling instrument. If such and such a phenomenon known in nature is followed by such another phenomenon known in nature, what will be the fourth phenomenon consequent on the third, which has been either provided by nature or imagined in imitation of nature? If the lance of an ordinary warrior is ten feet long, how long will the lance of Ajax be? If I can throw a stone weighing four pounds, Diomede should shift half a rock. The strides of the Gods and the bounds of their horses are in the imaginary ratio of Gods to men. It is the fourth note of the harmonic and is in proportion to the three others; from which the animal expects that resonance which always occurs in him, but which does not always occur in nature. The poet does not care, but it is none the less true for that. It is, however, quite different for the philosopher. He has next to interrogate nature, who often gives him a phenomenon quite different from what he had expected and then he perceives that his analogy has misled him.

D'Alembert: Well, good-bye, my friend, good-evening and good-night.

Diderot: You are joking now, but you will dream of our conversation on your pillow and if it does not take on consistency there, so much the worse for you: for you will be forced to adopt hypotheses of a far more ridiculous description.

D'Alembert: You are quite mistaken. I shall go to bed a sceptic. I shall rise a sceptic still.

Diderot: A sceptic! Can one be a sceptic?

D'Alembert: There you go again. Are you going to assert I am not a sceptic? Surely I am in the best position to know that I am one.

Diderot: Wait a moment.

D'Alembert: Be quick then. I am anxious for bed.

Diderot: I will be quite brief. Can you imagine a man finding his scale of strict logic exactly balanced for and against any proposition under discussion?

D'Alembert: No. That would turn one into Buridan's ass.*

Diderot: In that case there is no such thing as a sceptic, since with the exception of mathematical problems, which do not admit of the least uncertainty, there is a for and against in everything. The scales are never equal and it is impossible that they should not incline to the side which we think the most probable.

D'Alembert: But in the morning I see probability on the right, in the afternoon on the left.

Diderot: That is to say, that you are dogmatic for in the morning and dogmatic against in the afternoon.

D'Alembert: But in the evening when I realize the fleeting nature of my judgments, I believe none of them, neither those of the morning, nor those of the afternoon.

Diderot: That is to say, that you can no longer tell which of these conflicting opinions preponderated: that this preponderance appears too slight to base a fixed opinion upon it: and you choose to adopt the course of no longer busying yourself with such problematic subjects: of abandoning the discussion to others, and of never arguing about them any more yourself.

D'Alembert: That may be so.

* The donkey, invented by Jean Buridan, the Schoolman (1297–1358), which, pressed by both hunger and thirst, died of starvation and thirst, through being unable to choose between a measure of oats and a bucket of water.

Diderot: But if somebody pulled you aside, questioning you and in a friendly way asked you on your conscience to say on which of the two sides you found the fewest difficulties, would you be really and truly too embarrassed to answer and realize in your own person Buridan's ass?

D'Alembert: I suppose not.

Diderot: Come, my friend, if you think seriously you will find that in everything our real opinion is not the one about which we have never vacillated, but the one to which we have most often returned.

D'Alembert: I dare say you are right.

Diderot: And so do I. Good-night, my friend, and *memento quia pulvis es, et in pulverem reverteris.*

D'Alembert: A sad truth.

Diderot: And a necessary one. Allow man I do not say immortality, but only the double of his present term, and you will see what will happen.

D'Alembert: And what do you want to happen? And what does it all matter to me? Arrive what may, I want to go to sleep. Good-night!

D'ALEMBERT'S DREAM

Speakers: D'ALEMBERT, MLLE DE LESPINASSE,* DR. BORDEU.†

BORDEU: Well, then, what is the news? Is he ill?

MLLE DE LESPINASSE: I am afraid so. He had a very disturbed night.

BORDEU: Is he awake?

MLLE DE LESPINASSE: Not yet.

BORDEU (*after going up to D'Alembert's bed, and feeling his pulse and skin*): It won't be anything.

MLLE DE LESPINASSE: You think not?

BORDEU: I can answer for it. The pulse is good: a little weak . . . the skin damp, the breathing easy.

MLLE DE LESPINASSE: There is nothing to be done?

* Julie de Lespinasse, b. Lyon, 1732; d. Paris, 1776: illegitimate daughter of the Comtesse d'Albon. Till 1752 she lived in a state of dependence on her legitimate sister. She was rescued by Mme du Deffand, with whom she lived from 1753–1764. At this date she quarrelled with Mme du Deffand, and with the assistance of Mme Geoffrin she set up house for herself, where her salon became rapidly the most famous in Paris. For seven years she shared house with D'Alembert, perhaps without there being any physical relation between them. Diderot seems to suggest as much in his dialogue. In 1767 she left D'Alembert for the Marquis de Maura and him for the Comte de Guibert (see Marquis de Ségur's *Julie de L'Espinasse*, and *Correspondence de Julie de L'Espinasse*).

† Theophile de Bordeu, b. 1722 in the Basses Pyrenees, d. 1776 at Paris: a famous eighteenth-century doctor. Published, 1744, *Lettres sur les eaux minérales des Béarn;* 1752, *Traité des Glandes;* 1765, *Recherches sur le pouls par rapport aux cures;* 1775, *Recherches sur les maladies chroniques.* The opinions attributed to him by Diderot in this dialogue were not his. He was, on the contrary, a 'vitalist.'

Bordeu: Nothing.

Mlle de Lespinasse: That's a good thing, for he hates medicine.

Bordeu: And so do I. What did he have for supper?

Mlle de Lespinasse: He would not take anything. I do not know where he spent the evening, but he came back worried.

Bordeu. A slight attack of fever. There will be no complications.

Mlle de Lespinasse: On coming in he put on his dressing-gown and night-cap and threw himself into his armchair, where he fell asleep.

Bordeu: Sleep is good anywhere. But he would have been best in bed.

Mlle de Lespinasse: He lost his temper with Antoine, who told him so. He had to pester him for half an hour, to get him into bed.

Bordeu: That happens to me every day, though my health is good.

Mlle de Lespinasse: Once in bed, instead of lying quietly as usual, for he sleeps like a child, he began to turn and twist about, wave his arms, knock off his blankets, and talk out loud.

Bordeu: What did he talk about? Geometry?

Mlle de Lespinasse: No. It seemed to me pure raving. To begin with, some twaddle about vibrating strings and feeling fibres. It appeared to me so mad that I resolved not to leave him all night. Not knowing what to do, I moved up a little table to the foot of the bed, and I began to take down all I could catch of what he said in his sleep.

Bordeu: A good idea and just like you. Can I see it?

Mlle de Lespinasse: Easily. But I'll be hanged if you will make anything out of it.

Bordeu: That may be.

Mlle de Lespinasse: Listen: ". . . A living point. . . . No, I am mistaken. At first nothing, then a living point. . . . To this living point is applied another, then another; and from these successive applications results a being which is one, for I am one, there can be no doubt about that—(as he said that, he felt himself all over). But how is that unity made? ('But, my friend,' said I, 'what does that matter to you? Go to sleep.' He stopped talking. After a moment's silence he began again, as if addressing somebody) Stop a moment, philosopher, I can easily grasp an aggregate, a tissue of little feeling beings, but an animal! . . . a whole, a system, an itself, with consciousness of its own unity. I do not see it, no, I do not see it."

Doctor do you make anything of this?

Bordeu: A great deal.

Mlle de Lespinasse: You are very lucky. . . . "My difficulty springs perhaps from a false notion."

Bordeu: It is you who are talking?

Mlle de Lespinasse: No, the dreamer. To continue: He added, apostrophizing himself, "My friend D'Alembert, take good care, you are supposing only contiguity where there is really continuity. . . . Yes, he is sufficiently cunning to say that. . . . And the formation of this continuity? . . . That will hardly trouble him. . . . Just as one drop of mercury melts into another drop of mercury, one feeling, living molecule melts into another feeling, living molecule. . . . First there were two drops; after contact only one. Before assimilation there were two molecules; afterwards only one. . . . Feeling becomes common to the common-mass. And good gracious, why not? In my own mind I may distinguish as many parts as I please over the length of the animal fibres, but the fibre will be continuous, one . . . yes, one. . . . The contact of two homogeneous molecules, two perfectly homogeneous molecules forms continuity, and the most complete case of union, cohesion, combination, identity that can be imagined. Yes, philosopher, if these molecules are elementary and simple. But suppose they are aggregates, suppose they are compound? . . . The combination will take place none the less, and in consequence identity, continuity. And then the ordinary action and reaction. . . . It is certain that the continuity of two living molecules is quite another thing to the continuity of two passive masses. . . . Pass on, pass on! Perhaps I could quibble with you: but I do not care to; I am not a hair-splitter. . . . However, let's begin again. A thread of very pure gold. I remember it is a comparison he made. A homogeneous network, between the molecules of which others are interposed and form perhaps another homogeneous network, a tissue of feeling matter, *which assimilates on contact*, feeling, active here, passive there, which is communicated like movement, not to mention, as he very well said, that there must be some difference between the contact of two feeling molecules, and the contact of two molecules which are without feeling, and this difference, what can it be? . . . An habitual action and reaction . . . and this action and reaction of a character all their own. . . . Everything concurs, then, to produce a sort of unity which only exists in the animal. . . . Good heavens, if this is not the truth it is very like it." You are laughing, Doctor, can you find any sense in it?

BORDEU: Heaps.

MLLE DE LESPINASSE: He isn't mad then?

Bordeu: Not a bit.

Mlle de Lespinasse: After this preamble he began to cry out: "Mlle de Lespinasse, Mlle de Lespinasse!" "What do you want?" "Have you ever observed a swarm of bees escaping from their hive? . . . The world or the general mass of matter is the hive. Have you seen them go off and form at the end of the branch of a tree, a cluster of little winged animals, all clinging on to each other by the feet? This cluster is a being, an individual, an animal of sorts. . . . But these clusters should all be alike. . . . Yes, if matter had to be one and homogeneous. Have you seen them?" "Yes, I have seen them." "Have you seen them?" "Yes, friend, I say, yes." "If any one of these bees takes it into its head to sting in some way or other the bee to which it is attached, what do you think will happen? Tell me." "I don't know at all." "Still tell me. . . . You do not know then; but the philosopher, he knows. If you ever see him—and you will either see him, or not see him, for he gave me his word—he will tell you that the nearest one will sting the next, and that there will be stirred in all the clusters as many sensations as there are little animals, that the whole will be stirred and moved, and change shape and situation; that a noise will rise and little cries, and that any one who had never seen a cluster of this kind in action, might think it an animal with five or six hundred heads and a thousand or twelve hundred wings." Well, Doctor?

Bordeu: Well then, take my word for it, that this is a very fine dream and that you have done well to write it down.

Mlle de Lespinasse: Are you dreaming, too?

Bordeu: I am dreaming so little that I could almost promise to tell you what follows.

Mlle de Lespinasse: I defy you to.

Bordeu: You defy me?

Mlle de Lespinasse: Yes.

Bordeu: And if I meet your challenge?

Mlle de Lespinasse: If you meet it, I promise . . . I promise to take you for the greatest madman on earth.

Bordeu: Look at your paper and listen. The man who took this cluster for an animal would be mistaken. But, Mademoiselle, I presume that he continued talking to you. Do you wish him to make a saner judgment? Do you wish to transform the cluster of bees into a single unique animal? Soften their feet by which they hold together. Make them continuous instead of contiguous, which is what they were at first. Between this new state of the cluster and the former one there is certainly a marked difference, and what can the difference be except that what before was only a collection of animals is now a whole, a single animal? All our organs . . .

Mlle de Lespinasse: All our organs!

Bordeu: For one who has practised medicine and carried out a few observations. . . .

Mlle de Lespinasse: And then?

Bordeu: And then?—are only separate animals, which the law of continuity keeps in a general sympathy, unity, and identity.

Mlle de Lespinasse: I am amazed. That is what he said, almost word for word. So I can now assure the whole earth that there is no difference between a waking doctor and a dreaming philosopher.

Bordeu: It was already suspected. Is that everything?

Mlle de Lespinasse: Oh no, nowhere near. After your maunderings, or his, he said to me: " Mademoiselle—my friend?—come here—closer, closer; I have a suggestion to make to you." "What?" "Take hold of that cluster, there; you are sure it really is there?—make an experiment." "What experiment?" "Your scissors cut well." "Divinely." "Go up gently, quite gently, and separate these bees for me, but take care to cut them in the middle of their bodies, just at the place where they are made one by their feet. Don't be afraid. You will wound them a little, not kill them. Good. You are as neat as a fairy. See how they are flying off. Each to its own side. They are flying off one by one, two by two, three by three. How many there are! If you have understood me. . . . Have you understood me?" "Perfectly." "Suppose now—suppose . . ." Good gracious, Doctor, I understood so little of what I was writing: he spoke so low: this part of the paper is so muddled, that I cannot read it.

Bordeu: I will take up the tale, if you like.

Mlle de Lespinasse: If you can.

Bordeu: Nothing easier. Suppose these bees were so small, so small that their organisms continually eluded the gross edge of your scissors; you will go on dividing them as much as you like, but you will never kill any of them, and this whole, made up of imperceptible bees, will be quite a polypus, which you will kill only by crushing it. The difference between the continuous cluster of bees and the contiguous cluster of bees is precisely the difference between ordinary animals like ourselves or fishes on one side, and worms, serpents, and polypous animals on the other. This whole theory further undergoes certain modifications.

(*Here* Mlle de Lespinasse *gets up quickly and goes to pull the bell-rope.*)

Quietly, quietly, Mademoiselle. You will wake him up, and he needs rest.

Mlle de Lespinasse: I did not think of that. I was too dazed.

(*To the* Servant, *who comes in*)

Which of you went to the Doctor's?

Servant: I, Mademoiselle.

Mlle de Lespinasse: A long time ago?

Servant: I have got back less than an hour.

Mlle de Lespinasse: You did not take anything there?

Servant: Nothing.

Mlle de Lespinasse: Not a piece of paper?

Servant: No.

Mlle de Lespinasse: Very well. You may go. . . . I cannot get over it. Come, Doctor, I suspected one of them of having carried you my scrawl.

Bordeu: Nothing of the sort, I promise you.

Mlle de Lespinasse: Now I know your talent, you will be of the greatest use to me socially. But his dream did not stop there.

Bordeu: So much the better.

Mlle de Lespinasse: You see nothing alarming in all that?

Bordeu: Not in the least.

Mlle de Lespinasse: He continued: "Well, philosopher, you conceive polypi of every kind, even human polypi. But nature offers us no example of them."

Bordeu: Then he did not know about those two girls who were joined by the head, shoulders, back, buttocks, and thighs, who lived stuck together in this way till the age of twenty-three, and died within a few minutes of each other. And then he said?

Mlle de Lespinasse: The sort of thing you hear in madhouses. He said "that this has either happened already or will one day. And then who knows the state of affairs on the other planets ?"

Bordeu: One need not go so far as that perhaps.

Mlle de Lespinasse: "Human polypi in Jupiter or Saturn. Males dissolving into males, females into females. That's good." (Here he began to laugh so much that I was quite frightened.) "Man resolving into an infinity of atomic men, which one shuts up between sheets of paper as one does insects' eggs, which spin their shells, which remain a certain period in the chrysalis, which pierce their shells and escape as butterflies, and human society formed, an entire province peopled from the débris of a single man, a pleasant exercise for the imagination." (Then his fits of laughter began again.) "If man dissolves somewhere into an infinity of human animalculæ, we ought to mind death less: the loss of a man can be so easily repaired that he should not be much regretted."

Bordeu: This extravagant supposition is almost the real history of nearly all animals in existence or to come. If man does not resolve himself into an infinity of men, at any rate he resolves himself into an infinity of animalculæ whose metamorphoses it is impossible to foresee or their future and final organism. Who knows if this infinity of animalculæ is not the nursery of a second generation of beings, separated from the present one by an unimaginable interval of centuries and successive developments.

Mlle de Lespinasse: What are you mumbling about, Doctor ?

Bordeu: Nothing, nothing—I too was dreaming. Go on reading, Mademoiselle.

Mlle de Lespinasse: "Everything considered, however, I prefer our method of refilling the world," he added. "Tell me, philosopher, you who know what happens here, there, and everywhere, do not different parts of the body, when they have dissolved, produce men of differing character—the brain, the heart, the chest, the feet, the hands, the testicles? Oh! how that simplifies morality—a man born, a woman brought forth!" (Let me miss out this part, Doctor.) "A hot room furnished with little pots, and on each of these pots a label—warriors', magistrates', philosophers', poets', courtiers' pot, harlots' pot, kings' pot."

Bordeu: That is quite merry and mad. So this is called dreaming! It is a vision that recalls to my mind some very singular phenomena.

Mlle de Lespinasse: Then he began to mumble something about grains, strips of flesh left to soften in water, and different races of successive animals which he saw being born and dying out. He had imitated with his right hand the tube of a microscope and with his left, I think, the mouth of a vase. He looked into the vase by this tube and said: "Voltaire can laugh about it as much as he likes, but old Eely* is right. I believe my eyes: I see them. How many there are! How they come, how they go! How they frisk about!" He compared the vase in which he saw so many ephemeral generations to the universe: he saw the history of the world in a drop of water. This idea appeared to him a great one. He found it quite in accordance with sound philosophy, which studies great bodies in little ones. He said: "In Needham's drop of water,

* Nickname of Voltaire for the English physiologist and Catholic divine Needham [1713–1781]. He published in 1745 *An Account of some new Microscopical Discoveries founded on an Examination of the Calamary and its Wonderful Miltvessels*, a work in which he deduced a system of spontaneous generation from the study of cuttlefish. Hence Voltaire's nickname for him 'L'Anguillard.' Voltaire was enraged by work of apologetics he published in 1769 called *Recherches physiques et metaphysiques sur la nature de la religion*. Needham also endeavoured to read Egyptian hieroglyphics by means of Chinese characters. In 1764 his correspondence with Voltaire on miracles was published at Geneva, and was republished in London in 1769.

everything occurs and passes away in the twinkling of an eye. In the world the same phenomenon endures a little longer. But what is our duration compared with the eternity of time? Less than the drop of water which I have taken on the point of a needle, compared with the unlimited space which surrounds me. An indefinite succession of animalculæ in the fermenting atom, the same indefinite succession of animalculæ in the other atom, called the Earth! Who knows the races of animals which have gone before us? Who knows the races of animals that will come after our own? Everything changes, everything passes away. There is only the Whole which stays. The world begins and ends unceasingly: it is, every instant, at its beginning and its end. There has never been any other: and another there never will be.

In this vast ocean of matter, no one molecule is like another or is for an instant like itself. *Rerum novus nascitur ordo*. There is its eternal motto. Then he added with a sigh. "Oh the vanity of all our thoughts! Oh the trashiness of our glory and our works! O poverty! Oh the smallness of our views! There is nothing solid at all, but eating, drinking, living, loving, and sleeping! . . . Mlle de Lespinasse, where are you?" "Here." His face coloured. I wished to feel his pulse—but did not know where he had hidden his hand. He seemed to have a convulsion. His mouth was half open, his breath was hurried: he uttered a deep sigh: then a slighter one: then a deeper still. He turned his head again upon his pillow and fell asleep. I looked at him attentively; I was deeply moved without knowing why, my heart beating, and not with fear. After a few moments I saw a slight smile play over his lips. He said quite low: "In a planet where men multiplied like fish, where the spawn of a man pressed on the spawn of a woman—I should have few regrets. Mademoiselle, we must lose nothing that might be of use. Mademoiselle, if this could be collected in a flask and sent early one morning to Needham." Doctor, and you do not call this madness ?

Bordeu: Of course it is, when you are at hand.

Mlle de Lespinasse: Whether I am at hand or not makes no difference, and you do not know what you are talking about. I had hoped that the rest of his night would be peaceful.

Bordeu: That is certainly the usual consequence of what he had been doing.

Mlle de Lespinasse: Not a bit of it. At two in the morning he returned once more to his drop of water, which he called a mi . . . cro . . .

Bordeu: A microcosm.

Mlle de Lespinasse: That is the word he used. He admired the wisdom of the ancient philosophers. He said, or made his philosopher say, I do not know which of the two it was: " If, when Epicurus asserted that the earth contained the germs of everything, and that the animal species was the product of fermentation, he had offered to show on a small scale what happened on a large at the beginning of time, what would have been the answer ? . . . And you have this image under your eyes and it teaches you nothing ? . . . Who can tell if fermentation and its products are exhausted ? Who knows at what point we are in the succession of these animal generations ? Who knows if this deformed biped, little more than four feet high, still called a man near the Pole, and who would quickly lose that name by growing a little more deformed, is not the image of a passing species ? Who knows if this is not the case with all animal species ? Who knows if everything does not tend to reduce itself to a great passive immobile sediment ?

Who knows how long this passivity will last? Who knows what new race may some day spring from so great a mass of feeling, living points? Why not one single animal? What was the elephant originally? Perhaps the enormous animal it appears to us, perhaps an atom: both suppositions are equally possible. They only suppose movement and the diverse properties of matter. . . . The elephant, that enormous organized mass, the sudden product of fermentation! And why not? The relation of this great quadruped to its first womb is less close than that of the worm to the molecule of flour which produced it. . . . But the worm is only a worm. . . . You mean that its smallness, which hides its organism from you, takes away its wonder. But life, feeling, there is the wonder! And this wonder is one no longer. . . . When I have seen passive matter pass to the state of feeling, nothing can astonish me further. . . . What comparison can there be between a little number of elements fermenting in the hollow of my hand and this immense reservoir of divers elements, scattered in the bowels of the earth, on its surface, on the breast of the seas, in the spaces of the air! However, as the same causes subsist, why have the effects stopped? Why do we no longer see the bull pierce the earth with its horn, press its feet against the soil, and endeavour to release the dull weight of its body from it? . . . Allow the present race of existing animals to pass away. Let the great passive sediment act for a few million years. The renewal of the species will need, perhaps, a period ten times as long as that of its duration. Wait and be in no hurry to pronounce on the great work of nature. You have two chief phenomena, the passage from the passive state to the state of feeling and spontaneous generation. Let them be enough for you. Draw just conclusions from them, and in an order of things where nothing is in an absolute sense, big or small, lasting or transient, keep yourself clear of the sophism of the ephemeral. . . ." Doctor—what is this sophism of the ephemeral?

BORDEU: It is that of a transient being who believes in the immortality of things.

MLLE DE LESPINASSE: Fontenelle's rose, which said that within the memory of roses no gardener had been seen to die.

BORDEU: Precisely. That is graceful and profound!

MLLE DE LESPINASSE: Why do your philosophers not express yourselves with the grace of Fontenelle? Then we should understand you.

BORDEU: I am not certain that his frivolous tone suits serious subjects.

MLLE DE LESPINASSE: What do you call a serious subject?

BORDEU: Why, general feeling, the formation of the feeling being, its unity, the origin of animals, their duration, and all cognate questions.

MLLE DE LESPINASSE: And for myself, I call them lunatic subjects, which one may be allowed to dream about when asleep, but with which no sensible man will busy himself when awake.

BORDEU: And why, please?

MLLE DE LESPINASSE: Because some are so obvious that it is unnecessary to look for the reason, others so obscure that one can understand nothing about them, and all are completely useless.

BORDEU: Do you think, Mademoiselle, that it makes no difference whether one denies or admits the existence of a supreme intelligence?

MLLE DE LESPINASSE: No.

BORDEU: Do you think one can take sides about a supreme intelligence without knowing where one stands about the eternity of matter and its properties, the distinction of the two substances, the nature of man, and the generation of animals ?

Mlle de Lespinasse: No.

Bordeu: Then these questions are not as otiose as you said ?

Mlle de Lespinasse: But what is their importance to me if I can throw no light on them ?

Bordeu: But how should you know that you cannot if you do not examine them ? But may I ask you which are those problems which you find so clear that the examination of them appears to you unnecessary ?

Mlle de Lespinasse: That of my unity, of myself, for example. Good gracious, I don't find it necessary to waste so much breath in order to know that I am myself, that I have always been myself, and that I shall never be anybody else.

Bordeu: The fact is clear certainly, but the reason for the fact is the reverse, especially on the hypothesis of those who admit only one substance, and who explain the formation of man or animals in general by the successive apposition of several feeling molecules. Each feeling molecule has its 'myself' before being applied to something else. But how has it lost that 'myself' ? How as the result of all these losses has there resulted the consciousness of a whole ?

Mlle de Lespinasse: Contact, I think, is enough. Here is an experiment I have made a hundred times. . . . But wait, I must go and see what is happening behind the curtains. . . . He is asleep. When I put my hand on my thigh, I am at first quite aware that my hand is not my thigh, but a little time afterwards, when both are equally warm, I can no longer tell them apart. The limits of the two parts are confused and they are now one.

Bordeu: Yes, until one of the two is pricked by something—then the distinction is born again. There is then something in you which knows quite well if it is your hand or thigh that has been pricked, and that thing is not your foot—it is not even your pricked hand. It is your hand which is in pain, but it is something else which knows it, and which is not in pain itself.

Mlle de Lespinasse: I think it is my head.

Bordeu: All your head?

Mlle de Lespinasse: No, Doctor, now I am going to explain myself by a comparison. Comparisons are nearly always the arguments of women and poets. Imagine a spider.

D'Alembert: What is that? Is that you, Mlle de Lespinasse?

Mlle de Lespinasse: Keep quiet. (*Mlle de Lespinasse and the Doctor keep quiet a moment. Then Mlle de Lespinasse says in a low voice*) I think he has gone to sleep again.

Bordeu: No, I seem to hear something.

Mlle de Lespinasse: You are right. Has he begun dreaming again?

Bordeu: Listen.

D'Alembert: Why am I what I am? Because it was inevitable I should be. . . . Here, yes, but somewhere else? At the Pole? Under the Line? In Saturn? If a distance of some thousand leagues changes my species, what will the space of some thousands of terrestrial diameters not do? . . . And if everything is a general flux, as the spectacle of the universe everywhere teaches me, what will not be produced here and elsewhere by the passing and vicissitudes of some millions of centuries? Who can tell what the thinking and feeling being is in Saturn?

But is there feeling and thought in Saturn? Why not? Might the feeling and thinking being in Saturn have more senses than me? Ah, if so, the Saturnian is unfortunate. The more the senses, the more the needs!

Bordeu: He is right. Organs produce needs, and reciprocally needs produce organs.*

Mlle de Lespinasse: Are you raving too, Doctor?

Bordeu: But why not? I have seen two stumps become in time two arms.

Mlle de Lespinasse: That is not true.

Bordeu: It is. To make up for two arms which were missing I have seen shoulder-blades grow longer, move tweezer-wise and become two stumps.

Mlle de Lespinasse: What madness!

Bordeu: It is a fact. Suppose a long succession of armless generations, suppose continuity of effort, and you will see the two sides of these tweezers stretch out, stretch out further and further, cross behind the back, come back again in front, perhaps grow fingers at the ends, and re-form arms and hands. The original conformation grows worse or better by necessity and normal functioning. We walk so little, we toil so little, and think so much, that I do not despair of man ending up by being only a head.

Mlle de Lespinasse: A head, a head! That is a very small matter. I hope that reckless gallantry. . . . You put ridiculous ideas into my head. . . .

Bordeu: Hush!

D'Alembert: So I am what I am, because I had to be. Change the whole, and of necessity you change me. But the whole changes unceasingly. Man is only a common result, the freak a rare one, both equally

* Diderot probably found these Lamarckian ideas in the writings of Robinet, whose *De la Nature* had appeared in 1761.

natural, equally necessary, equally in the universal general order of things. . . . And what is there astonishing in that? All beings circulate one within the other: consequently all species. . . . Everything is in perpetual flux. . . . Every animal is more or less a man, every mineral more or less a plant. . . . There is nothing precise in nature. . . . The ribbon of Father Castel. . . .* Yes, Father Castel, it is your ribbon and nothing more. Everything is more or less one thing or another, more or less earth, more or less water, more or less air, more or less fire: more or less of one kingdom or another. . . . So nothing is quintessentially a particular being—certainly not—since there is no quality in which no being participates . . . and it is the greater or lesser proportion of this given quality which makes us attribute it to one being as opposed to another. . . . You speak of individuals, poor philosophers! Leave your individuals out. Is there in nature an atom exactly like another? No. Do you not agree that everything holds together in nature and that there cannot be a link missing in the chain? Then what do you want to get at with your individuals? There is no such thing, no, no such thing. . . . There is only one great single individual. There is the Whole. In this whole, as in a machine, or any sort of animal, there is a part which you call by such and such a name. But when you give the name *individual* to this part of the whole, your concept is as false as if, in a bird, you gave the word *individual* to the wing or to the feather of a wing. . . . And you talk of essences; poor

* Père Bertrand Castel [1680–1751] was the supposed inventor of an 'ocular clavecin,' in which the notes produced coloured ribbons to represent all their nuances. Diderot makes further references to Père Castel in his *Letter on Deaf-mutes*. Père Castel published several works on mathematics and optics. His 'ocular clavecin' is described in his *Nouvelles experiences d'optique et d'acoustique* (1735).

philosophers, leave your essences out. Look at the general mass, or if your imaginations are too narrow to grasp it, consider your first origin and your latter end. . . . O Architas, you who measured the globe, what are you now ? A little ash. What is a being ? . . . The sum of a certain number of tendencies. Can I be anything else than a tendency ? No, I go to a determined end. And species ? Species are but tendencies to the common term, which is proper to them. And life ? Life, a succession of actions and reactions. . . . Living, I act and react in mass. . . . Dead, I act and react in molecules. . . . I do not die then ? No, doubtless in that sense I do not die, neither myself nor anything that is. What matters one shape or another ? Birth, life, and death are just changes of shape. And what does one shape or another matter ? Each has the happiness and misery proper to it. From the elephant to the aphis . . . from the aphis to the feeling, living molecule, the origin of all things, there is no point in the whole of nature which does not feel pain or pleasure.

Mlle de Lespinasse: He has stopped.

Bordeu: Yes. But his excursus was a fine one. There is lofty philosophy for you. I am for the moment a man of systems, and I believe the more human knowledge advances the more this philosophy will turn out true.

Mlle de Lespinasse: And we, where were we ?

Bordeu: Upon my word, I do not remember. He recalled to me, as I listened, such a quantity of phenomena.

Mlle de Lespinasse: Stop! Stop! I was at my spider.

Bordeu: So you were.

Mlle de Lespinasse: Draw up, Doctor. Imagine a spider in the middle of its web. Break a thread and you will see that alert creature come running up. Well, suppose the threads, which the insect pulls out of his intestines and recalls at will, were a feeling part of himself?

BORDEU: I understand. You imagine somewhere in yourself, in a nook of your head, the nook called the membrane, for example, one or several points to which all the sensations excited along the length of the threads are referred.

MLLE DE LESPINASSE: You have it.

BORDEU: Your notion is as just as possible, but do you not see that is almost the same as a certain cluster of bees?

MLLE DE LESPINASSE: That is so. I talked prose without knowing it.

BORDEU: And excellent prose, too, as you are going to see. He that only knows man in the shape he presents to us at birth knows nothing at all about him. His head, his feet, his hands, all his limbs, all his viscera, all his organs, his nose, his eyes, his ears, his heart, his lungs, his intestines, his muscles, his bones, his nerves, his membranes are nothing, properly speaking, but the coarse developments of a network, which forms itself, increases, spreads, and throws out a multitude of imperceptible threads.

MLLE DE LESPINASSE: There you have my web. And the original point of all these threads is my spider.

BORDEU: Exactly so.

MLLE DE LESPINASSE: Where are the threads? Where is the spider placed?

BORDEU: The threads are everywhere. There is no point on the surface of your body to which they do not lead, and the web is tucked away in a part of the head which I have named to you, the membrane which I could hardly touch without reducing the whole machine to torpor.

Mlle de Lespinasse: But if an atom disturbs one of the threads of the spider's web, then the spider takes fright, grows agitated, makes off or runs up to help. In the centre she is instructed of what happens in any part of the great room she has furnished. Why is it that I do not know what passes in my own room or the world since I am a ball of feeling points and that everything presses on me and I on everything?

Bordeu: Because impressions grow feebler in proportion to the distance from which they start.

Mlle de Lespinasse: If someone hits as gently as possible the end of a long beam, I hear the blow if my ear is at the other end. If this beam touched Earth at one end and Sirius at the other, the effect would be the same. Why, when everything is linked together and contiguous—that is to say, the beam is existent and real—why do I not hear what is going on in the immense space that surrounds me—above all, if I listen attentively?

Bordeu: And who says you do not hear more or less? But it is so far off, the impression of it is so feeble, it is so often crossed on the way by other impressions, that you are surrounded and deafened by the quantity of violent and diverse noises: for between Sirius and you bodies are only contiguous where they ought to be continuous.

Mlle de Lespinass: What a pity.

Bordeu: Yes, indeed. For otherwise you would be God. By your identity with all the beings in nature you would know everything that is happening. And through your memory everything that has already happened.

Mlle de Lespinasse: And everything that is going to happen?

Bordeu: You would form very plausible conjectures about the future, but they would be liable to error, just as if you tried at the end of your foot or hand to divine what was going to happen inside you.

Mlle de Lespinasse: And how do you know this world has not also its membrane, or that there does not reside in some nook of space a large or small spider whose threads spread everywhere?

Bordeu: I do not know; and still less that there has not been one in the past or will not be in the future.

Mlle de Lespinasse: Could a god like that one . . .

Bordeu: The only conceivable kind.

Mlle de Lespinasse: . . . have existed in the past or come into being and passed away?

Bordeu: Certainly. Since he would be matter in the universe, part of the universe, subject to vicissitudes, he would grow old and die.

Mlle de Lespinasse: And now another extravagance has come into my head.

Bordeu: You need not tell it me. I know what it is.

Mlle de Lespinasse: Well then, what is it?

Bordeu: You see intelligence allied to very energetic portions of matter, and the possibility of every conceivable sort of prodigy. Others have thought like you.

Mlle de Lespinasse: You have guessed right, and I think none the better of you for it. You must have a wonderful leaning towards madness.

Bordeu: Agreed. But what is there terrible in this idea? There would be an epidemic of good and evil geniuses: the most constant laws of nature would be interrupted by natural agencies: our general system of physics would become more difficult: but there would be no miracles.

Mlle de Lespinasse: One must really be very careful about what one asserts and what one denies.

Bordeu: Come. The man who described to you a phenomenon of this kind would appear to be a tremendous liar; but leave out these imaginary beings, including your spider with its infinite networks. Come back to your own network and its formation.

Mlle de Lespinasse: Certainly.

D'Alembert: Mademoiselle, you have somebody there. Who is it talking to you?

Mlle de Lespinasse: It's the Doctor!

D'Alembert: Good-morning, Doctor, what are you doing here so early?

Bordeu: You shall be told later. Go to sleep now.

D'Alembert: And really I need it. I do not think I have ever passed such a disturbed night as this one. You will not go before I am up.

Bordeu: No. I'll swear, Mademoiselle, you thought that as you were at the age of twelve a woman half your present size, at the age of four half the size again, as fœtus a small woman, in the ovaries of your mother a very small woman, you thought you had always been a woman in your present shape, so that it was only your successive increases in size which have made the difference between what you were originally and what you are to-day.

Mlle de Lespinasse: I agree.

Bordeu: Nothing, however, is falser than this notion. First you were nothing. You were, to begin with, an imperceptible point, formed of smaller molecules, scattered in the blood, the lymph of your father and mother. This point becomes a loose thread, then a bundle of threads. Up to now, not the least vestige of your present agreeable form, your eyes, those beautiful eyes no more resemble eyes than the end of an anemone's stalk resembles an anemone. Each of the ends of the bundle of threads transformed itself simply by nutrition and conformation into a special organ, after allowing for the organs into which the ends of the bundle are changed and the organs to which they give birth. The bundle is a purely feeling system; if it subsisted in this form, it would be susceptible to all impressions relative to pure feeling, as cold, heat, softness, roughness. These successive impressions, different from each other and differing in intensity, would produce, perhaps, memory, consciousness of self, very limited reasoning power. But this feeling, pure and simple, this touching is varied by organs emanating from each of these ends: an end, by forming an ear, gives birth to a kind of touch which we call noise or sound. Another, by forming the palate, gives birth to a second kind of touch which we call taste; a third, forming the nose and covering it up, gives birth to a third kind of touch which we call smell. A fourth, by forming an eye, gives birth to a fourth kind of touch which we call colour.

Mlle de Lespinasse: But if I understand you aright, those who deny the possibility of a sixth sense, or a real hermaphrodite, rush on too quickly. Who told them that nature could not form a bundle with a peculiar end that would give birth to an organ which is unknown to us?

Bordeu: Or with the two ends which characterize the two sexes? You are right. It is really pleasant to talk with you. You not only understand what one says to you, but you deduce therefrom consequences of an astonishing soundness.

Mlle de Lespinasse: You say that to encourage me, Doctor.

Bordeu: On my honour, no! I say what I think.

Mlle de Lespinasse: I quite see how some of the ends of the bundle are employed. But the others, what happens to them ?

Bordeu: Do you think anybody but yourself would have thought of that question ?

Mlle de Lespinasse: Of course they would.

Bordeu: That shows you are not vain. The rest of the ends go to form as many other kinds of touch, as there is diversity between the organs and the parts of the body.

Mlle de Lespinasse: And what are they called ? I have never heard of them.

Bordeu: They have not got a name.

Mlle de Lespinasse: Why not ?

Bordeu: Because there is not as much difference between the sensations excited by means of them as there is between the sensations excited by means of the other organs.

Mlle de Lespinasse: You quite seriously think that the foot, the hand, the thighs, the belly, the stomach, the chest, the lungs, the heart have their private sensations ?

Bordeu: I think so. If I dared, I should ask you if among those sensations one does not talk about. . . .

Mlle de Lespinasse: I quite understand. No. That one is all of a piece; and a great pity it is. What is your reason for supposing the existence of this multiplicity of sensations, more painful than agreeable, with which you are good enough to endow us ?

Bordeu: The reason ? Because we can in a great measure discern them. If this infinite diversity of touching did not exist, one would know that one felt pleasure or pain, but one would not know to what to attach them. One would need the help of sight.

It would no longer be an affair of sensation, but one of experiment and observation.

Mlle de Lespinasse: On my saying I had a pain in my finger, if asked why I assert that it is my finger that is in pain, I should have to answer not that I feel it to be so, but that I feel a pain and perceive that my finger is suffering.

Bordeu: That is it. Come and let me kiss you.

Mlle de Lespinasse: I shall be delighted.

D'Alembert: Doctor, you are kissing Mademoiselle. Fine goings on!

Bordeu: After a great deal of thought, I have reached the conclusion that the direction in which the shock lay and the place of the shock would not be sufficient to determine such a rapid judgment on the part of the origin of the bundle.

Mlle de Lespinasse: I do not know at all.

Bordeu: Your doubt is delightful. So many people take for natural qualities habits which have been acquired and are almost as old as ourselves.

Mlle de Lespinasse: And reciprocally too.

Bordeu: However that may be, you see that in a question which concerns the first formation of the animal, it is beginning too late to fix one's regard and thoughts on the formed animal. We must go back to the first rudiments: and it is as well to despoil you of your present organism and return to the moment when you were only a soft substance, fibrous, shapeless, wormlike, more analogous to a bulb or the root of a plant than to an animal.

Mlle de Lespinasse: If it were the custom to walk naked in the streets, I should be neither the first nor the last to conform. So make anything you like of me provided I gain information. You told me that each end of the bundle formed a special organ. What is the proof of that?

Bordeu: Do in your mind's eye what nature sometimes does. Deprive the bundle of one of its ends. What do you think will happen?

Mlle de Lespinasse: The animal will have no eyes perhaps.

Bordeu: Or only one in the middle of its forehead

Mlle de Lespinasse: A Cyclops, in fact.

Bordeu: Yes, a Cyclops.

Mlle de Lespinasse: Then perhaps the Cyclops was not necessarily fabulous.

Bordeu: So little so that I will let you see one, whenever you want to.

Mlle de Lespinasse: Who knows the reason of this variation?

Bordeu: Why, the man who dissected this monster and found he had only one optic thread. Do in your mind's eye what nature does sometimes. Suppress another end of the bundle, the end that should form the nose, and the animal will be noseless. Suppress the end which should form the ear, the animal will have no ears or only one, and the anatomist will find, when he is dissecting, neither olfactory nor auditive threads, or will find only one of them. Continue the suppression of the ends and the animal will be headless, footless, handless; his duration will be short, but he will have lived.

Mlle de Lespinasse: Are there examples of that?

Bordeu: Most assuredly. But that is not all. Double some of the ends of the bundle and the animal will have two heads, four eyes, three testicles, three feet, four arms, or six fingers on each hand. Upset the arrangement of the ends of the bundle, and the organs will be in the wrong place. The head will be in the middle of the chest, the lungs on the left and the heart on the right. Stick two ends together and the organs will be muddled up. The arm will get attached to the body: thighs, legs, and feet will join together, and you will have every conceivable sort of freak.

Mlle de Lespinasse: But it seems to me that such a compound machine as an animal—a machine which springs from a point, from a stirring fluid, perhaps from two fluids mixed at random, for one scarcely knows what happens—a machine which advances to perfection by an infinity of successive developments—a machine whose regular or irregular formation depends on a packet of thin threads, all loose and flexible, on a sort of skein where the smallest thread cannot be broken, burst, put in the wrong place or missing without disastrous consequences for the whole—such a machine must surely tie itself up and get into difficulties on the scene of its formation more often than the silks on my winder.

Bordeu: It does suffer far more inconvenience than one thinks. But there has not been enough dissection, and our ideas on its formation are very far from the truth.

Mlle de Lespinasse: Have we any striking examples of these deformities at the origin, besides hump-backs and cripples, whose unhappy state we might attribute to some hereditary taint?

Bordeu: Innumerable ones. Just lately there has died in the Paris workhouse at the age of twenty-five, from inflammation of the lungs, a carpenter born at Troyes called Jean-Baptiste Macé, who had the internal viscera of the chest and the abdomen transposed; the heart on the right side exactly as yours is on the left: the liver on the left: the stomach, the spleen, and the pancreas in the right hypochonder: the portal vein to the liver on the left side, although it belongs to the liver on the right side: the same transposition all along the intestinal canal: the kidneys, backing along the vertebræ of the loins, looked like a horseshoe. And now let people come and talk to us of final causes.

Mlle de Lespinasse: How extraordinary!

Bordeu: If Jean-Baptiste Macé has married and had children . . .

Mlle de Lespinasse: These children, Doctor . . .

Bordeu: Will have the ordinary conformation. But some one of their children's children after a century (for these irregularities go by jumps) will return to the fantastic conformation of its ancestor.

Mlle de Lespinasse: And to what are these jumps due?

Bordeu: Nobody knows. It takes two to make a child, as you know. Perhaps one of the agents repairs the taint of the other; the defective network only reappears at the moment when the descendant of the freakish race is in the predominance and gives the law to the formation of the network. The bundle of threads constitutes the first organic difference between all species of animals. Variations in the bundle of one species account for all the freakish variations of that species.

(*After a long silence* Mlle de Lespinasse *awakes from her reverie and pulls the Doctor out of his own by the following question*):

I have a quite mad notion.

Bordeu: What is it?

Mlle de Lespinasse: Man is perhaps only the freak of a woman or woman of a man.

Bordeu: You would have had this notion much more quickly had you known that a woman has all the organs of a man and that the only difference between them is one has a bag hanging outside and the other has it tucked away inside: that the male and female fibres are so alike as to be easily mistaken: that the part which causes the mistake to be made grows proportionately smaller in the female fœtus as the interior purse grows larger: that it is never obliterated to the point of losing its first shape: that it keeps this shape on a small scale: that it can go through the same movements: that it is also the prime mover of pleasure: that it has its gland and its prepuce, and that one observes at its extremity a point which would seem to have been the orifice, since closed up, of a urinary canal: that there is in man from the anus to the scrotum a space known as the perineum, and from the scrotum to the extremity of the penis a raphe which seems to correspond to the frenulum clitoridis; that women with the clitoris overdeveloped grow beards: that eunuchs do not have any: that their thighs grow broader, their haunches larger, their knees rounder: that, in losing the characteristic organism of one sex, they seem to hark back to the characteristic conformation of the other. Those Arabs who have been castrated by continual riding lose their beards, develop a high voice, dress as women, sit with them in their chariots, and affect their habits and customs. But we are a long way from our subject. Let us come back to our bundle of animated, living filaments.

D'Alembert: I think you are talking filth to Mlle de Lespinasse.

Bordeu: When talking science, one must supply technical terms.

D'Alembert: You are right. And then they lose the band of associated ideas which would make them coarse. Go on, Doctor. So you said to Mademoiselle that the womb is nothing else than a scrotum turned outside in, a movement in the course of which the testicles have been thrown out of the bag which shut them in and dispersed right and left in the cavity of the body: that the clitoris is the male organ on a small scale. That this male organ in a woman gets smaller and smaller as the womb or tucked-back scrotum increases, and that . . .

Mlle de Lespinasse: Yes, yes, be quiet: and don't meddle in our affairs.

Bordeu: You see, Mademoiselle, that for our sensations in general, which are only variations on touch, one must leave on one side the successive forms the network takes and stick to the network itself.

Mlle de Lespinasse: Each thread of the feeling network can be hurt or tickled along all its length. Pleasure or pain is here or there, in one place or another, of one of those long spider's legs of mine, for I always come back to my spider. It is the spider which is the common starting-point of all the legs and which relates pain and pleasure to such and such place though it does not feel them.

Bordeu: It is this power of constantly and invariably referring all impressions back to this common starting-point which constitutes the unity of the animal.

Mlle de Lespinasse: It is the memory of all these successive impressions which makes for each animal the history of its life and self.

Bordeu: And it is the memory and comparison which follow necessarily from all these impressions which make up thought and reasoning.

Mlle de Lespinasse: And where is this comparison made?

Bordeu: At the origin of the network.

Mlle de Lespinasse: And this network?

Bordeu: Has back at the origin no sense proper to it. It does not see, does not hear, suffers no pain. It is produced and nourished: it emanates from a soft, unfeeling, passive substance, which serves it as a pillow and on which it sits, hears, judges, and pronounces.

Mlle de Lespinasse: It feels no pain.

Bordeu: No. The slightest disturbance suspends its audience: and the animal falls into a state of death. Stop the disturbance and it resumes its functions and the animal is born again.

Mlle de Lespinasse: And how do you know that! Has anyone ever made a man be born and die at will?

Bordeu: I am going to tell you. It is a curious fact. La Peyronie,* whom you may have known, was called to the bedside of a patient who had received a violent blow on the head. The patient felt a throbbing there. The surgeon had no doubt that an abscess had been formed on the brain, and that there was not a moment to lose. He shaves the patient and trepans him. The point of the instrument penetrates right into the middle of the abscess. The pus had collected: he empties out the pus: he cleans the abscess with a syringe. When he pushes the injection into the abscess the patient closes his eyes. His limbs remain without action, without movement, without the least sign of life. When he pumps the injection out again and relieves the origin of the bundle of the weight and pressure of the injected fluid, the patient, reopening his eyes, moves, speaks, sees, feels, is reborn, and lives.

Mlle de Lespinasse: How extraordinary! And the patient got better?

Bordeu: Yes. He got better. And when he was better, he reflected, he thought, reasoned, had the

* Surgeon [1678–1747] to Louis XV, who in 1731 created at his request the Academy of Surgery.

same cast of mind, the same good sense, the same penetration as before with a fair part of his brain gone.

Mlle de Lespinasse: This judge of yours is an extraordinary creature.

Bordeu: He too makes mistakes at times. He is subject to prejudice born of habit. We feel pain in a limb we have got no longer. You can cheat him if you will. Cross two of your fingers one on the top of another and touch a little ball. He will say there are two balls.

Mlle de Lespinasse: He is like all other judges. He must have experience or else he will mistake the feeling of ice for that of fire.

Bordeu: He does quite another thing. He gives almost indefinite volume to the individual, or he concentrates himself almost into a point.

Mlle de Lespinasse: I don't understand.

Bordeu: What is it that circumscribes your real space, the real sphere of your feeling ?

Mlle de Lespinasse: My sight, my touch.

Bordeu: By day, yes. But what about the night, in the dark, when you dream, especially on some abstract subject: and even by day, when your mind is occupied.

Mlle de Lespinasse: Nothing does. I exist as in a point. I almost cease to be matter, I only feel my thought. There is no longer place, movement, body, distance, or space for me. The universe is wiped out for me, and I am nothing for it.

Bordeu: There is the final term to the concentration of your existence. But its ideal expansion can be boundless. When too much strain has been put on your sensibility either in the way of your being drawn together and condensed within yourself, or of being stretched outwards, no one knows any longer what may happen.

Mlle de Lespinasse: Doctor, you are right. It has seemed to me several times in dreams . . .

Bordeu: And to people suffering from an attack of gout . . .

Mlle de Lespinasse: . . . that I became immense.

Bordeu: . . . that their feet touched heaven from their bed. . . .

Mlle de Lespinasse: That my arms and legs grew infinitely longer, and that the rest of my body took on a proportionate volume. That the Enceladus of the fable was only a pigmy: that the Amphitrite of Ovid, whose long arms went to form a mighty belt round the earth, was only a dwarf compared with me: that I scaled the heavens and embraced the two hemispheres.

Bordeu: Very good. And I know a woman in whom the phenomenon occurred the other way on.

Mlle de Lespinasse: What? She grew gradually smaller and returned into herself?

Bordeu: Till she felt herself as small as a needle. She saw, she heard, she reasoned, she judged: she was mortally afraid of losing herself. She shuddered at the approach of the smallest objects. She did not dare budge from where she was sitting.

Mlle de Lespinasse: What an extraordinary dream, most tiresome and inconvenient!

Bordeu: She was not dreaming. It was an accident caused by the cessation of the period.

Mlle de Lespinasse: And did she remain a long time in this tiny imperceptible shape of a midget?

Bordeu: One hour, two hours. After that she came gradually back to her natural volume.

Mlle de Lespinasse: And what is the reason for these fantastic sensations?

Bordeu: In their natural calm state the ends of the bundle have a certain tension, a tone, a regular energy, which circumscribes the size, real or imaginary, of the body. I said real or imaginary, because this tension, this tone, this energy being variable, our body is not always of the same volume.

Mlle de Lespinasse: And so in physics as in ethics we are liable to think ourselves bigger than we are.

Bordeu: Cold shrinks us, heat expands us, and a man may think himself all his life smaller or larger than he really is. If the mass of the bundles happens to get violently excited, the ends to stand on end and the infinite multitude of their extremities to rush forward beyond their accustomed limits, then the head, the feet, the other limbs, all points of the surface of the body, will be pulled out an immense distance and the person will feel like a giant. The contrary phenomenon will occur if feelinglessness, apathy, passivity seize the extremities of the strands and proceed bit by bit to the starting-point of the bundle.

Mlle de Lespinasse: I quite see that this expansion would be immeasurable. I quite see, too, that this feelinglessness, this apathy, this passivity of the extremity of the ends, this torpor, after making a certain amount of progress, would get fixed and stop.

Bordeu: As happened to La Condamine. Then the person feels as if there were balloons under his feet.

Mlle de Lespinasse: He exists beyond the limit of his own feeling; and if he were enveloped on every side by this apathy, he would offer us the sight of a little living man under a dead man.

Bordeu: You may conclude from that that the animal, which was originally only a point, still does not know if he is really anything more. But let us come back.

Mlle de Lespinasse: Where?

Bordeu: Where? Why, to La Peyronie's trepan. That is, I think, what you asked me for, the case of a man who lived and died alternately. . . . But we can go one better.

Mlle de Lespinasse: And what can that be?

Bordeu: The fable of Castor and Pollux made actual: two children; when one began to live, the other immediately died: similarly when the first one died, the second began to live.

Mlle de Lespinasse: A pretty story. And did that last long?

Bordeu: Their time of life was two days, which they shared equally and in turns, so that each had for its share one day's life and one day's death.

Mlle de Lespinasse: I am afraid, Doctor, that you are trying to abuse my credulity. Take care. If you deceive me once, I shall never believe you again.

Bordeu: Do you ever read the *Gazette de France?*

Mlle de Lespinasse: Never, though it is the masterpiece of two brilliant men.*

Bordeu: Get someone to lend you the number for the fourth of this month, September, and you will see that at Rabastens in the diocese of Albi two girls were born back to back, joined together by the last vertebræ of their loins, their thighs, and the hypogastric region. It was impossible to hold one upright without the other being upside down. When lying down, they faced each other. Their thighs were twisted between their trunks and their legs were raised up. In the middle of the common circular line, which attached them by their hypogasters, their sexual organs were visible, and between the right thigh of one which

* Arnaud and Suard, editors from 1765.

corresponded to the left thigh of her sister, in a cavity, there was a little anus, from which meconium flowed.

Mlle de Lespinasse: That's a very fantastic species.

Bordeu: They took milk, which was given them in a spoon. They lived twelve hours, as I told you, one falling into a collapse, as the other emerged from it, one dead while the other was living. The first collapse of one and the first life of the other lasted four hours. Afterwards the alternating collapses and returns to life lasted less long: they both died at the same moment. It was observed that their navels had also an alternating movement of egress and ingress, ingress in the case of the one who collapsed and egress for the one who was returning to life.

Mlle de Lespinasse: And what have you to say about these alternations of life and death?

Bordeu: Nothing worth saying, perhaps. But as people see everything through the glass of their theory, and I do not wish to be an exception to the rule, I hold that this is the same phenomenon as the man trepanned by La Peyronie, duplicated into two beings who were joined together: that the networks of these two children were so mixed that they acted and reacted on each other. When the origin of the network of one of them prevailed it involved the network of the other, which immediately collapsed. The contrary occurred when the network of the second dominated their common system. In the case of the man trepanned by La Peyronie, the pressure was affected from top to bottom by the weight of a fluid. In the case of the twins of Rabastens, it was effected from bottom to top by the traction of a certain number of the network's threads; this conjecture is supported by the alternating ingress and egress of the navels, egress in that which returned to life, ingress in that which died.

Mlle de Lespinasse: So there were two souls bound together.

Bordeu: Rather an animal which had, in theory, two senses and two consciousnesses.

Mlle de Lespinasse: But who could only enjoy one of them at any given moment. Who can say what might have happened had the animal lived?

Bordeu: What sort of relation would the experience of every moment of life, the strongest of conceivable habits, have established between these two brains?

Mlle de Lespinasse: Double senses, a double memory, a double imagination, double powers of application, one half observing, reading, meditating, while the other half is in repose, this second half taking on the same functions when its comrade is tired. Life doubled by a double being.

Bordeu: That is possible; and as nature produces in time all possible things she will form some strange compound.

Mlle de Lespinasse: What poor creatures we should be in comparison with such a being!

Bordeu: But why? So many uncertainties, contradictions, and follies already occur with a single understanding that I have no idea what might happen with a double one. . . . But it is half-past ten and I can hear a patient who is calling me all the way from the Faubourg here.

Mlle de Lespinasse: Would it be very dangerous for him if you did not see him?

Bordeu: Less dangerous, perhaps, than if I did. If nature does not do the work without me, we shall have great difficulty in doing it together, and it is quite certain I shall not do it alone.

Mlle de Lespinasse: Stay here then.

D'Alembert: Doctor, one word more and I send you off to your patient. How comes it that I have remained myself to myself and others through all the vicissitudes I have undergone in the course of my life, and when perhaps I possess no longer a single one of the molecules I brought with me at my birth?

Bordeu: You have told us in your dream.

D'Alembert: Did I have a dream?

Mlle de Lespinasse: All night, and it was so like delirium that I sent to fetch the doctor this morning.

D'Alembert: And all that for the spider's legs, which took alarm of themselves, kept the spider on the alert, and made the animal talk. And what did the animal say?

Bordeu: That he was himself to others and to himself through the functioning of memory and, I would add, by the slowness of the changes. Had you passed in the twinkling of an eye from youth to decrepitude, you would have been thrown on the world as at the first moment of your birth. You would have no longer been yourself to yourself and to others, who would not in turn have been themselves to you. All relations would have been destroyed, all the history of your life would have been confused to me, and all mine to you. How could you have known that this man, bent upon his stick, whose eyes were dimmed, who dragged himself along with pain, more different from himself inside even than outside, was the same as he who yesterday strode along so lightly, moved such heavy weights, and could give himself over to such profound meditations, to the gentlest as to the most violent exercises? You would not have understood your own works; you would not have recognized yourself; no one would have recognized you. All the world's scene would have changed. Consider that there was less difference between yourself at birth and yourself when young than there would be between yourself when young and yourself grown suddenly decrepit. Consider that, though your birth has been linked to your youth by a series of uninterrupted sensations, the first three years of your life have never made part of your life's history. What, then, had your youth been to you, had nothing linked it to the moment of your decrepitude? D'Alembert decrepit would have had not the least recollection of D'Alembert young.

Mlle de Lespinasse: In the cluster of bees not one would have had time to take on the " spirit " of the cluster.

D'Alembert: What is that you are saying?

Mlle de Lespinasse: I say that the spirit of a monastery is conserved because the monastery re-peoples itself bit by bit, and, when a new monk enters, he finds a hundred old ones who lead him on to think and feel like them. A bee goes away and another succeeds him in the cluster and quickly makes himself at home.

D'Alembert: Come, come, you are waxing extravagant with your monks, your bees, your cluster, and your convent.

Bordeu: Not so extravagant as you might think. Though there be only one consciousness in animals, there is an infinity of wills. Each organ has its own.

D'Alembert: What quite did you say?

Bordeu: I said that the stomach wished for food, that the palate did not: that the difference between the palate and the stomach on one side and the whole animal on the other is just that the animal knows what he wants, but the stomach and palate want without knowing. In fact, stomach and palate stand in much the same relationship as man to brute. Bees lose their consciousness and retain their appetites or wills.

Fibre is a simple animal, man a compound one. But let us reserve this subject for another time. A far smaller event than decrepitude can take from a man the consciousness of himself. A dying man receives the sacraments with deep piety: he admits his faults: he asks pardon of his wife, he embraces his children: he calls in his friends: he speaks to his doctor: he gives orders to his servants: he dictates his final wishes: he puts his affairs in order: and he does all this with the soundest judgment and with complete use of his faculties. He gets better; he is convalescent; he has not the slightest idea of what he said or did during his illness. This interval of time, which may be a very long one, has disappeared from his life. There are cases known of persons taking up the conversation or the action at the point where they had been interrupted by the sudden attack of illness.

D'Alembert: I remember that, during a public lecture, a college pedant, all puffed up with his knowledge, was what they call "downed" by a Capucin he had despised. He, downed! And by whom? By a Capucin! And what about? About contingent eventualities and divine prescience—a subject which he had thought about all his life; and under what circumstances? Before a large company!—before his pupils! He sees his honour gone! His head is so obsessed by these ideas that he falls, as a result, into a lethargy, which deprives him of all the knowledge he had acquired.

Mlle de Lespinasse: That was a good thing anyhow.

D'Alembert: Upon my word, you are right His natural senses were left, but he had forgotten everything. He was taught to speak and read again, and died as he was learning to spell quite nicely. This man was by no means a fool. He was even allowed some measure of eloquence.

Mlle de Lespinasse: As the doctor has listened to your story, he must now listen to mine. A young man from eighteen to twenty years old—I do not recall his name——

Bordeu: It was a M. Schullemburg de Wirterthour; he was only fifteen or sixteen.

Mlle de Lespinasse: This young man had a fall which left him with a violent commotion in the head.

Bordeu: What is your idea of a violent commotion? He fell from the top of a barn: his head was cracked and he was unconscious for six weeks.

Mlle de Lespinasse: However that may be, do you know the results of the accident? The same as with your pedant—he forgot everything he knew. He returned to childhood: he had a second infancy, and it lasted. He was timid and cowardly, and was amused by toys. If he had been naughty and was scolded, he went and hid in a corner: he asked leave to pay a big or a little visit. He was taught to read and to write, but I forgot to tell you he had to be taught to walk all over again. He became a man again, and a clever man; and he has left a book of natural history.

Bordeu: No. They are engravings, the plates for M. Zulyer on Insects, arranged on the plan of Linnæus. I knew about it: it happened in the canton of Zurich in Switzerland, and there are many similar examples. Disturb the origin of the bundle, and you will change the animal. The whole thing seems there, sometimes dominating the ramifications, sometimes dominated by them.

Mlle de Lespinasse: And the animal submits either to despotism or anarchy.

Bordeu: To despotism—just the word. The origin of the bundle commands, and all the rest obeys. The animal is master of himself, *mentis compos*.

Mlle de Lespinasse: And to anarchy when all the ends of the network rise against their chief, and there is no supreme authority.

Bordeu: Perfect. In moments of great passion, in delirium, at times of imminent peril, if the master directs all the forces of his subjects to one point, the feeblest animal will show incredible strength.

Mlle de Lespinasse: During the vapours a kind of anarchy peculiar to us.

Bordeu: These vapours are the image of a feeble administration, where each claims for himself the authority of the master. I know only one means of cure. It is difficult, but certain. The origin of the feeling network, that part which constitutes one's self, has to be induced by some very strong motive to recover its authority.

Mlle de Lespinasse: What happens then ?

Bordeu: Authority is recovered or the animal dies. If I had the time, I would tell you two curious facts about that.

Mlle de Lespinasse: But, Doctor, it is now too late for your appointment. Your patient is no longer expecting you.

Bordeu: One should only come here when one has nothing to do, for one can't get away.

Mlle de Lespinasse: Well, that's a polite way of being rude. But what about your stories ?

Bordeu: For to-day, you must content yourself with one. A woman fell, after childbirth, into an appalling state of vapours. Nothing but tears and involuntary laughs, chokings, swellings in the throat, gloomy silence, piercing cries, and all the worst things possible. That lasted several years. She was passionately in love and thought she saw that her lover, who was becoming wearied by her illness, was beginning to lose his affection for her. Then she resolved to be cured or to perish. A civil war raged in her, in which sometimes the master prevailed, sometimes the subjects. If the action of the ends of the network happened to equal the reaction of the origin, she fell down as though dead. She was carried to her bed, where she remained hours together motionless and almost lifeless. At other times she was seized with attacks of lassitude, with a general collapse, with an extinction, which seemed inevitably final. She persisted six months in this state of struggle. The revolt always began with the threads. She felt it coming on. At the first symptoms she got up, ran about, gave herself up to the most violent exercises: she rushed up and down stairs: sawed wood; dug the earth. The organ of her will, the origin of the bundle, grew stronger. She said to herself: Victory or Death. After an infinite number of victories and defeats, the chief remained master, and the subjects became so obedient that, though this woman has experienced all sorts of domestic troubles and has suffered from different illnesses, there has never been any further question of the vapours.

Mlle de Lespinasse: That is fine. But I think I should have done as much.

Bordeu: Yes, because if you loved at all, you would love a great deal and you have a strong character.*

Mlle de Lespinasse: I understand. One has a strong character, if by habit or organism the origin of the bundle dominates the threads. A weak one, on the other hand, if it is dominated by them.

Bordeu: There are other consequences to be deduced from that.

Mlle de Lespinasse: But your other story, and then the deductions.

* This presumably refers to the fact that Mlle de Lespinasse was, in spite of everything, not in love with D'Alembert.

Bordeu: A young woman had rather kicked over the traces. One day she decided to shut her door on pleasure. She is alone, melancholy, vaporous. She sent for me—I advised her to wear peasant's dress, to dig all day, sleep on straw, and eat stale bread. The regime did not please her: "Travel then," I said. She made the tour of Europe and regained her health on the high road.

Mlle de Lespinasse: That is not what you had to tell me. No matter, come to your consequences.

Bordeu: There would be no end to it.

Mlle de Lespinasse: So much the better: go on.

Bordeu: I have not got the courage.

Mlle de Lespinasse: Why not?

Bordeu: Because at the rate we are going, we touch on everything and get to the bottom of nothing.

Mlle de Lespinasse: No matter. We are talking, not writing theses.

Bordeu: For example, if the origin of the bundle attracts all forces to itself, if the whole system moves backwards, so to speak, as happens, I think, with the man who is meditating deeply, with the fanatic who sees the heavens opened, with the savage who sings amid the flames, in cases of ecstasy, and voluntary or involuntary alienation . . .

Mlle de Lespinasse: Well?

Bordeu: Well. The animal makes himself insensitive—he only exists at one point. I have not seen that priest of Calame of whom Saint Augustine speaks, who alienated himself to the point of no longer feeling burning coals. I have not seen on the spot those savages who smile on the enemies who insult them and suggest to them tortures more exquisite than any they have been made to undergo. I have not seen in the circus those gladiators who dying recalled their gracefulness and lessons in gymnastics. But I believe all these facts, because I have seen, yes, seen with my own eyes an effort as astonishing as any of these.

Mlle de Lespinasse: Do tell it me, Doctor. I am like a child and love marvellous stories, and, when they reflect credit on the human species, it is but rarely I question their truth.

Bordeu: There was in a little town in the Champagne, Langres, a worthy curé, called Le or de Moni, thoroughly penetrated and imbued with the truth of religion. He was afflicted with a stone which had to be cut out. The day was chosen, the surgeon, the assistants, and myself go to his house: he receives us serenely, he undresses, he gets into bed. We wish to tie him down. He refuses. "Only put me," he says, "in the right position." He is put in it. Then he asks for a large crucifix, which was at the foot of the bed. He is given it and he clasps it in his arms, he presses it to his lips. He is operated upon, he remains motionless; there escape from him neither tears nor sighs, and he was delivered of the stone without being aware of it.

Mlle de Lespinasse: That is fine, and now can you doubt that the man, whose chest-bones were broken with stones, saw the heavens open?

Bordeu: Do you know what ear-ache is?

Mlle de Lespinasse: No.

Bordeu: So much the better for you. It is the cruellest of all pains.

Mlle de Lespinasse: Worse than tooth-ache, with which I am acquainted unfortunately?

Bordeu: Incomparably so. A philosopher friend of yours had been tormented by it for a fortnight, when one morning he said to his wife: "I do not feel I have the courage to get through the day. . . ." He thought his only resource was to cheat the pain by artifice. Little by little, he dug himself so deeply into some question of metaphysics or geometry that he forgot all about his ear. He was served with food, which he ate without noticing. He got through till bedtime without having had any pain. The terrible agony began again only when the contention in his mind had stopped, but this time its fury was unparalleled, either because fatigue had actually aggravated the pain or because weakness rendered it more intolerable.

MLLE DE LESPINASSE: In emerging from such a state, one must certainly be worn out with fatigue. That is what sometimes happens to that man there.

BORDEU: That is dangerous. He should take care.

MLLE DE LESPINASSE: I never stop telling him so; but he takes no notice.

BORDEU: He is no longer the master. It is his life. He must inevitably die of it.

MLLE DE LESPINASSE: Really, you quite frighten me.

BORDEU: What does this wearing out, this exhaustion, prove? That the ends of the bundle have not remained idle, and that throughout the whole system a violent tension has been directed towards a common centre.

MLLE DE LESPINASSE: And suppose this tension or violent tendency lasts, suppose it becomes habitual?

BORDEU: It is a tic on the origin of the bundle. The animal is mad and mad without remedy.

MLLE DE LESPINASSE: And why?

BORDEU: Because a tic in the origin is not the same as a tic on one of the ends. The head can easily command the feet, but not the feet the head: the origin can command one of the ends, but not the end the origin.

Mlle de Lespinasse: And the difference, please? But why can I not think all round a subject? That is a question which should have occurred to me earlier.

Bordeu: Ah, because consciousness is only in one place.

Mlle de Lespinasse: So my question is easily answered.

Bordeu: But it can be only in one place, in the common centre of all sensations, there where the memory is, there where comparisons are made. Each end can take in but a determined number of impressions or sensations which are successive, isolated, without memory. The origin can take in all impressions: it registers them, it keeps the memory, or continuous sensation, of them, and the animal is induced from its earliest formation to relate itself there, of itself to fix itself completely there, to exist there.

Mlle de Lespinasse: And if my finger could have memory?

Bordeu: Your finger would think.

Mlle de Lespinasse: And what is memory then?

Bordeu: The property of the centre, the specific sense of the origin of the bundle, as sight is the property of the eye. And it is no more astonishing that memory is not in the eye than it is that sight is not in the ear.

Mlle de Lespinasse: Doctor, you rather elude my questions than answer them satisfactorily.

Bordeu: I elude nothing; I tell you what I know, and I should know more if the organization of the origin of the network was as well known to me as that of the end, if I had had the same facilities for observing it. But though I am weak at particular phenomena, I triumph in general phenomena.

Mlle de Lespinasse: And what are these general phenomena?

Bordeu: Reason, judgment, imagination, madness, imbecility, ferocity, instinct.

Mlle de Lespinasse: I understand. All these qualities are but the consequences of the relations, either original or contracted by habit, between the origin of the bundle and its ramifications.

Bordeu: Precisely. Is the principal or trunk too vigorous relatively to the branches? Thence spring poets, artists, men of imagination, timid men, enthusiasts, madmen. Is it too weak? Thence come what are called brutes, savage beasts. Perhaps the whole system is cowardly, soft, and devoid of energy. Then you get imbeciles. Or energetic, in perfect accord, well ordered. Then you get powerful thinkers, philosophers, sages.

Mlle de Lespinasse: And to the tyrant branch which happens to predominate is due the diverse instincts of animals, the diverse genius of men: the smelling power of dogs, the hearing of fish, the sight of eagles. D'Alembert is a mathematician, Vaucanson an engineer, Grétry a musician, Voltaire a poet. These are the differences consequent on one end in the bundle being more vigorous than any other, and than the similar end in creatures of the same species.

Bordeu: And also the habits which rule them: the old man, who still loves women, and Voltaire, who still writes tragedies.

(*At this point the Doctor began to dream, and* Mlle de Lespinasse *said to him*):

Mlle de Lespinasse: Doctor, you are dreaming.

Bordeu: I am.

Mlle de Lespinasse: What about?

Bordeu: Voltaire.

Mlle de Lespinasse: Well?

Bordeu: I was dreaming about the way in which great men are made.

Mlle de Lespinasse: And how are they made?

Bordeu: How feeling. . . .

Mlle de Lespinasse: Yes, feeling?

Bordeu: Or the extreme mobility of certain threads of the network is the dominating characteristic of second-rate people.

Mlle de Lespinasse: Doctor, what blasphemy!

Bordeu: I expected that. But what is a man of feeling? One who is a prey to the discretion of the diaphragm. Has a touching word struck his ear, a singular phenomenon struck his eye, note the internal tumult which arises all of a sudden, all the ends of the bundle stirred, the shudder which spreads, the horror which seizes, the tears which flow, the sighs which choke, the voice which interrupts, the origin of the bundle which does not know what is happening: no more coolness, no more reason, no more judgment, no more instinct, no more resourcefulness.

Mlle de Lespinasse: It is the picture of me.

Bordeu: The great man, if by ill-chance he has received this disposition from nature, will work unceasingly to weaken it, to dominate it, to make himself master of his movements and to keep the origin of the bundle secure in all its authority. Then he will be self-possessed amid the greatest dangers: he will judge coldly but sanely. Nothing will escape him of what will serve his views and help towards his object. He will not be easily surprised; he will be forty-five, a great king, a great minister, a great statesman, a great artist, above all a great actor, a great philosopher, a great musician, a great doctor. He will reign over himself and all his surroundings. He will have no fear of death, that fear, which as the Stoic has sublimely said, is the handle the strong man seizes to lead the feeble whither he will. He will have broken the handle, and will have freed himself at the same moment from all the tyrannies of the world. The men of feeling or madmen are on the stage. He is in the stalls. It is he who is the wise man.

Mlle de Lespinasse: Heaven defend me from the society of your wise man!

Bordeu: It is through not having tried to resemble him that you will be a prey to violent pains and pleasures in alternation, that you will divide your time between laughter and tears and never be more than a child.

Mlle de Lespinasse: I am resigned to that.

Bordeu: And you expect to be the happier for it?

Mlle de Lespinasse: I know nothing about that.

Bordeu: Mademoiselle, this quality which you prize so much and which leads to nothing great, never operates strongly without your feeling pain or is in abeyance without your being bored. You either yawn or are intoxicated. You give yourself up immoderately to the sensation of delicious music: you let yourself be involved in the charm of a delicious scene. Your diaphragm tightens, the pleasure has passed, and nothing is left but a choking which lasts all the evening.

Mlle de Lespinasse: But suppose I can enjoy the sublime music or the touching scene only on this condition?

Bordeu: That is where you make your mistake. I can also enjoy, I can admire, and I never suffer pain unless it be from colic. I have unmixed pleasure. My censure is more grave, my praise more flattering, and the result of more reflexion. Can there be such a thing as a bad tragedy for souls as mobile as your own? How many times have you not blushed, on reading a play, at the transports you underwent in the theatre, and *vice versa*?

Mlle de Lespinasse: Yes, that has happened to me.

Bordeu: It is not then for the person of feeling like you, it is for the calm, cold person like me to say: "That is true, that is good, that is beautiful." Strengthen the origin of the bundle. That is the best thing we can do. Do you know life itself is at stake?

Mlle de Lespinasse: Life. But that is serious, Doctor.

Bordeu: Yes, life. There is no one who is not sometimes disgusted with it. A single event is enough to render this sensation involuntary and habitual: then, despite distractions, varied amusements, the advice of friends, or one's own efforts, the ends obstinately deal their deathly blows to the origin of the bundle. It is no use for the poor wretch to struggle: the universe grows blacker to him. He walks with a band of melancholy notions which never leave him, and he finishes by casting off the burden of himself.

Mlle de Lespinasse: Doctor, you terrify me.

D'Alembert: And sleep, Doctor, what do you say about that? It is a good thing.

Bordeu: Sleep, that state in which, be it lassitude or habit, all the network is relaxed and remains motionless, in which, as in illness, each thread of the network is stirred, moves, transmits to the common origin a crowd of sensations often incongruous, disconnected, confused: at other times, so bound together, so connected, so well ordered that the waking man could be no more reasonable, eloquent or imaginative: at times so violent and so vivid that the waking man is uncertain as to their reality.

Mlle de Lespinasse: Well then, sleep?

Bordeu: . . . is a state of the animal in which there is no more ensemble. All concerted action, all discipline ceases. The master is abandoned to the discretion of his vassals and to the unbridled force of his own activity. Is the optic thread agitated? Then the origin of the network sees. It hears if the auditive thread demands it. Action and reaction are the only things which subsist between them. This is consequent on the central property, on the law of continuity and habit. If the action begins by the voluptuous end which nature has destined for the pleasure of love and the propagation of the species, the effect of the reaction on the origin of the bundle will be to reveal the image of the beloved. If this image, on the other hand, is first of all revealed to the origin of the bundle, the tension of the voluptuous end, the effervescence and effusion of the seminal fluid will be the effect of the reaction.

D'Alembert: So there is a dream which goes up the threads, and a dream which comes down them. I had one of the two to-night. But I do not know which road it took.

Bordeu: In the waking state, the network obeys the impressions made by an external object. Asleep it is from the exercise of its own feeling that everything passing within itself emanates. There is nothing to distract in a dream, hence its vivacity. It is almost always the result of an erethism, a passing attack of illness. The origin of the bundle is in this case alternately active and passive, in an infinity of different ways: hence its disorderly state. The concepts are sometimes as closely connected, or as distinct, in these cases, as if the animal were actually confronted with an object in nature. The dream is only the image of this object called up again. Hence its truthfulness, hence the impossibility of distinguishing it from the state of waking. Neither of these states is more probable than the other, and there are no means of perceiving the error but by experiment.

Mlle de Lespinasse: And can experiment always be effective?

Bordeu: No.

Mlle de Lespinasse: If my dream offers me the sight of a friend whom I have lost, offers it to me as convincingly as if my friend existed: if he speaks to me and I hear him: if I touch him and he creates the impression of solidity in my hands: if on waking my soul is full of tenderness and grief and my eyes bathed in tears, if my arms are still stretched towards the spot where he appeared to me, what will assure me that I have not in truth seen, heard, and touched him?

Bordeu: His absence. But if it be impossible to tell sleep from waking, who shall judge of the dream's length? In tranquil states, it is an interval stuffed in between the moment of going to bed and that of getting up. In troubled conditions, it lasts sometimes years. In the first case at least the consciousness of self entirely ceases. Could you tell me of a dream no one ever has had, or ever will have?

Mlle de Lespinasse: Yes, a dream in which you dream you are somebody else.

D'Alembert: And in the second case, one has not only consciousness of self, but one has consciousness of one's will and one's liberty. What is this liberty, what is this will of the dreamer?

Bordeu: What is it? Why the same as that of the waking man, the latest impulsion of desire and aversion; the latest result of everything one has been from one's birth to the actual instant—and I defy the subtlest mind to see the least difference there.

D'Alembert: Do you think so?

Bordeu: Is it you who put that question? You who, given over to profound speculations, have passed two-thirds of your life dreaming with your eyes open and acting without willing! Yes, without willing, even less than in your dream. In your dream, you commanded, you gave orders, you were obeyed: you were discontented or satisfied, you met with contradiction, you lost your temper, you loved, you hated, you blamed, you came and went. In the course of your meditations, your eyes were scarcely open in the morning before, when again seized upon by the idea which had occupied you yesterday, you put on your clothes, sat down at your table, meditated, traced figures, followed up calculations, dined, took up your equations again, sometimes left the table to verify them, spoke to other people, gave orders to your servant, had supper, went to bed, went to sleep—all without having performed the least act of the will. You have been only a point: you have acted, but you have not willed. Does one will spontaneously? Will is always born of some internal or external motive, of some present impression, or some past reminiscence, of some passion, or some plan for the future. After that, I will only say one word about liberty—that the least of our actions is the necessary effect of one cause, one . . . ourselves, very complicated, but one.

Mlle de Lespinasse: The necessary effect?

Bordeu: Certainly. Try to imagine the occurrence of some other action with the actor remaining the same.

Mlle de Lespinasse: He is right. Since I act thus and thus, the person who can act otherwise is no longer myself: and to say that, at the moment when I do or say a thing, I might say or do something else, is to assert that I am myself and somebody else at the same time. But, Doctor, what about vice and virtue? Virtue, that word which is holy in every language, that idea which is so sacred to every people.

Bordeu: We must change the word into Beneficent actions and Mischievous actions. One is born with a fortunate or an unfortunate disposition, and is irresistibly involved in the general current, which leads one person to glory and another to disgrace.

Mlle de Lespinasse: And self-respect, shame, remorse?

Bordeu: Puerilities founded on ignorance and the vanity of a person, who imputes to himself the merit or demerit of an inevitable instant.

Mlle de Lespinasse: And rewards and punishments?

Bordeu: They are means of correcting the malleable being one calls wicked and encouraging the one called good.

Mlle de Lespinasse: Is not this doctrine rather dangerous?

Bordeu: Is it true or false?

Mlle de Lespinasse: True, I think.

Bordeu: So you think that falsehood has its advantages and truth its inconveniences.

Mlle de Lespinasse: I do.

Bordeu: So do I. But the advantages of falsehood are momentary, those of truth everlasting: the inconvenient consequences of truth, when there are any, pass away quickly, while those of falsehood finish only with the falsehood. Look at the effects of falsehood on the mind of man, and its effects on his conduct. In his mind, either the lie is more or less connected with truth, and his mind is in a muddle, or it is thoroughly and consistently imbued with falsehood, and his mind is sunk in error. Well, what sort of conduct can you expect from a mind which is either inconsistent in its reasoning or consistent in its errors?

Mlle de Lespinasse: The second vice, though less despicable, is perhaps more dangerous than the first.

D'Alembert: Very good. So everything comes back to feeling, memory, organic movements; I more or less agree. But what about imagination, abstraction?

Bordeu: Imagination . . .

Mlle de Lespinasse: One moment, Doctor; let us recapitulate. Following your principles, it seems to me that by a succession of purely mechanical operations, I could reduce the greatest genius on earth to a mass of unorganized flesh, which would be left with a capacity to feel only during isolated moments. Then I could restore this shapeless mass, which is in the deepest state of conceivable stupidity, to the condition of the man of genius. One of these phenomena would consist in depriving the original skein of a certain number of its ends and of mixing the rest all up: the inverse phenomenon consists in restoring to the skein the ends one has detached and in abandoning the whole to a fortunate development. For example, I take from Newton the two auditive ends, and he has no more sensation of noise: the two olfactory ends and he has none of smell: the optic ends and he has none of colour: the palate ends and he has no sensation of taste. I suppress or mix up the others, and farewell to the organism of the brain, memory, judgment, desires, aversions, passions, will, consciousness of self, and we are left with a shapeless mass, which has retained only life and feeling.

Bordeu: Two almost identical qualities. Life has the quality of an aggregate, feeling of an element.

Mlle de Lespinasse: I take up this mass again and I restore to it its olfactory ends—it smells: its auditory ends, and it hears: its optic ends, and it sees: its palate ends, and it tastes. In straightening out the rest of the skein, I allow the other ends to develop, and I see the rebirth of memory, comparisons, judgment, reason, desires, aversions, passions, natural aptitude, talent, and I find my man of genius again, and that without the interference of any heterogeneous and unintelligible agent.

Bordeu: Perfect. Hang on to that. The rest is mere twaddle. . . . But abstractions? But imagination? Imagination is the memory of shapes and colours. The sight of a scene or of an object necessarily strings the feeling instrument in a certain way. It either strings itself or is strung by some outside cause. Then it trembles inside or resounds outside. It records to itself in silence the impressions it has received or it scatters them by means of recognized sounds.

D'Alembert: But in the account it gives, it exaggerates, omits circumstances or adds to them, disfigures the fact or beautifies it, and the feeling instruments near by conceive impressions which are certainly those of the resounding instrument, but not of the thing which has happened.

Bordeu: That is true; the account is historical or poetical.

D'Alembert: But how is this poetry or falsehood introduced into the account?

Bordeu: By the ideas, which are associated one with the other, and these ideas are set working because they have always been connected. As you have taken the liberty to compare the animal species to a clavecin, you must allow me to compare the poet's account to song.

D'Alembert: That is only fair.

Bordeu: There is in every song a scale. This scale has its intervals: each note has its harmonic, and these harmonics have theirs. Then there is introduced into the melody modulations as it goes along, and the song is enriched and broadened. The fact is a given motif, which each musician feels in his own way.

Mlle de Lespinasse: And why confuse the issue by using this figured style? I should say that everyone with eyes in his head sees, and describes what he sees, differently. I should say that each idea calls up others, and that according to one's turn of mind or character one either holds on to the ideas that severely represent the fact or one introduces into it associated ideas. I should say there is a choice between these ideas. I should say that this subject alone, if adequately treated, would furnish matter for a book.

D'Alembert: You are right. But that will not stop my asking the doctor if he is quite certain that a shape which resembled nothing could never be bred in the imagination and could not be produced in the account of it.

Bordeu: I think I am. The perversion of this faculty reduces itself to the skill of those charlatans, who, from several dismembered animals, construct a freak, which has never been seen in nature.

D'Alembert: And abstractions?

Bordeu: There are none. There are only habitual reticences, ellipses which make propositions more general and language more rapid and more convenient. For the abstract sciences had their origin in the symbols of language. A quality common to several actions has bred the words vice and virtue: a quality common to several beings has bred the words ugliness and beauty. People said one man, one horse, two animals: people then said, one, two, three, and the whole science of numbers was born. People had no idea of an abstract word. They observed three dimensions in all bodies—length, breadth, thickness: they got to work on these three dimensions: thence all mathematical sciences arose. Every abstraction is but a sign void of an idea. The idea has been excluded by separating the sign from the physical object, and it is only by reattaching the sign to the physical object that science becomes once more a science of idea: hence the need, so frequent in conversation and in books, of getting down to examples. When, after a long combination of signs, you ask for an example, you are demanding from the speaker nothing save that he give body, shape, reality, idea, to the successive noises of his tone of voice by applying to them sensations already experienced.

D'Alembert: Is that quite clear to you, Mademoiselle?

Mlle de Lespinasse: Not entirely, but the Doctor is going to explain.

Bordeu: You are good enough to say so. It may well be there is something to rectify, and much to add to, in what I have said. But it is 11.30 and at 12 I have a consultation in the Marais.

D'Alembert: You said: "The most rapid and convenient language!" Doctor, does one ever understand? Is one ever understood?

Bordeu: Almost all conversations are statements of fact. Wherever is my stick? There is no idea present in the mind. . . . And my hat? And for the very good reason that no man resembles another perfectly, we never understand precisely, we are never precisely understood. There is the bit more or the bit less in everything. Our speech always lags behind or goes beyond the sensation. We perceive a great deal of diversity in judgments made, but there are a thousand diversities we do not perceive and fortunately could not perceive. . . . Good-bye, good-bye.

Mlle de Lespinasse: One word more, I implore you.

Bordeu: Quick then, quick !

Mlle de Lespinasse: You remember those jumps you spoke to me about.

Bordeu: Yes.

Mlle de Lespinasse: Do you think that fools and clever people have these jumps in their blood ?

Bordeu: Why not ?

Mlle de Lespinasse: So much the better for our great-nephews. Perhaps a Henri IV will reappear.

Bordeu: Perhaps he has reappeared already.

Mlle de Lespinasse: Doctor, you must come back and dine with us.

Bordeu: I will do what I can, I can't promise. Expect me when you see me.

Mlle de Lespinasse: We will wait till two.

Bordeu: Excellent.

THE CONVERSATION CONTINUED

Speakers: Mlle de Lespinasse *and* Bordeu.

About two o'clock, the Doctor came back. D'Alembert *had gone out to dine, and the Doctor found himself tête-à-tête with* Mlle de Lespinasse. *Dinner was served. They talked about more or less trifling things till the dessert, but, when the servants had gone,* Mlle de Lespinasse *said to the Doctor:*

Mlle de Lespinasse: Come, Doctor, take a glass of malaga, and then you will answer a question which has worried me a hundred times, but which I should dare put to you alone.

Bordeu: An excellent malaga. But your question?

Mlle de Lespinasse: What do you think of the mingling of species?

Bordeu: And, upon my word, a very good question too. I think that men have attached a great deal of importance to the act of generation and that there they have been right. But I am dissatisfied with their laws, be they civil or religious.

Mlle de Lespinasse: And what do you find to urge against them?

Bordeu: That they have been drawn up without fairness, without object, and without any regard for the nature of things or for the needs of the public.

Mlle de Lespinasse: Try and explain.

Bordeu: That is my object. But, stop. (*He looks at his watch.*) I have still a good hour at your disposal. I shall travel quickly and there will be plenty of time. We are alone, you are not a prude, you will not imagine I wish to fail in the respect I owe you; and, whatever be the opinion you may hold of my ideas, I hope for my part that you will conclude nothing against the purity of my morals.

Mlle de Lespinasse: Certainly not. But your opening alarms me.

Bordeu: In that case, we will change the subject.

Mlle de Lespinasse: No, no, go on. One of your friends, who was looking out for husbands for myself and my two sisters, advised a sylph for the youngest, a great Angel of the Annunciation for the eldest, and a disciple of Diogenes for me. He knew us all three well. But still, draw a veil, Doctor, a thin veil.

Bordeu: Of course, as far as the subject and my calling admit.

Mlle de Lespinasse: Oh, that will not inconvenience you. But there is your coffee—take your coffee.

Bordeu (*after taking his coffee*)*:* Your question includes physics, ethics, and poetry.

Mlle de Lespinasse: Poetry!

Bordeu: Of course. The art of creating beings who do not exist in imitation of those that do is true poetry. This time, instead of Hippocrates, you will allow me to quote Horace. This poet or artisan says somewhere *Omne tulit punctum qui miscuit utile dulci:* the highest merit consists in having combined the agreeable and the useful. Perfection consists in conciliating these two qualities. An action both agreeable and useful must occupy the first place in the æsthetic order: we cannot refuse the second place to the useful: the third place goes to the agreeable: and we will relegate to the last row that which affords neither pleasure nor profit.

Mlle de Lespinasse: Up to now I can be of your opinion without blushing. But where will it lead us?

Bordeu: You will see. Mademoiselle, could you tell me what profit and what pleasure chastity and severe continence afford either to the individual who practises them or to society?

Mlle de Lespinasse: In truth, none.

Bordeu: And so, despite the magnificent eulogia fanaticism has showered on them, in spite of the civil laws which protect them, we will scratch them off the catalogue of virtues, and will agree that there is nothing so puerile, so ridiculous, so absurd, so harmful, so despicable, nothing worse, with the exception of positive evil, than these two rare qualities.

Mlle de Lespinasse: We can allow that.

Bordeu: Take care. In a moment, I warn you, you will be retracting.

Mlle de Lespinasse: We never retract.

Bordeu: Then actions performed in solitude?

Mlle de Lespinasse: Well?

Bordeu: Well. They afford, at least, pleasure to the individual and our principle is false or . . .

Mlle de Lespinasse: What, Doctor?

Bordeu: Yes, Mademoiselle, yes, and for the reason that these actions are not so unprofitable. It is a need and, even if one were not driven on by the need, the thing is always agreeable. I wish people to be healthy, I wish it without qualification, do you understand? I blame all excess, but, in a state of society like our own, there are a hundred reasonable considerations on its side without counting temperament and the disastrous consequences of severe continence—above all, for young people. Shortage of money, the fear men have of an agonizing repentance, among women the fear of dishonour, all of which lead an unhappy creature dying of languor and boredom, a poor devil who does not know to whom to address himself, to relieve himself in the manner of the cynic. Cato said to a young man about to call on a courtesan: "Courage, my child." Would he say the same thing to-day? If, on the contrary, he caught him alone and red-handed, would he not add: "That's better than corrupting someone else's wife or risking one's honour and health"? Goodness me, because circumstances deprive me of the highest pleasure imaginable, that of mingling my senses with the senses of the companion my heart has chosen, my passion with her passion, my soul with her soul, and in reproducing myself in her, and with her, because I cannot consecrate my action with the seal of usefulness, shall I forbid myself a necessary and delightful moment? One is bled to relieve the plethora; and what signifies the nature of the superabundant humour, and its colour, and the manner of its deliverance? It is just as superfluous in one of these indispositions as in the other. And if, after being pumped up again from its reservoirs and distributed through all the machine, it is evacuated by a longer and more painful and dangerous road, will it be any the less lost? Nature tolerates nothing useless. And then can I be blameworthy in helping her, when she calls for my help by the least equivocal of symptoms? Let us never provoke her, but occasionally lend her a hand: in refusal and idleness I see nothing but stupidity and loss of pleasure. "Live simply," I shall be told, and "tire yourself out." I understand. I must inflict on myself pain in order to ward off pleasure. A very happy notion!

Mlle de Lespinasse: That is a doctrine that should not be preached to children.

Bordeu: Nor to anyone else. But allow me a supposition. You have a daughter, virtuous, too virtuous; innocent, too innocent: and of an age when the temperament develops. Her head swims, nature does not help her. You call me in. I perceive at once that all the symptoms which are alarming you spring from the superabundance and the retention of the seminal fluid: I warn you she is threatened with a kind of madness, which it is difficult to prevent and which it is sometimes impossible to cure. I indicate the remedy. What will you do?

Mlle de Lespinasse: To tell you the truth I think . . . But the case never arises.

Bordeu: Undeceive yourself. It is by no means rare, and would be quite common if the looseness of our morals did not prevent it. . . . However that may be, merely to divulge these principles would be to trample decency under foot, to bring down on one's own head the most odious suspicions, and to commit a crime of *lèse-société*. But you are wandering.

Mlle de Lespinasse: Yes, I was uncertain whether to ask you if you have ever found yourself in the situation of having to make such a confidence to mothers.

Bordeu: Certainly.

Mlle de Lespinasse: And what point of view did they adopt?

Bordeu: All, without exception, the right, the sensible point of view. . . . I should not take my hat off in the street to a man suspected of practising my doctrine. Sufficient for me that he was called a scoundrel. But now there are no witnesses to our talk, nor consequences springing from it, and I will say to you about my philosophy what Diogenes, when quite stripped, said to the young and bashful Athenian, with whom he was preparing to wrestle: "Fear nothing, my son, my bark is worse than my bite."

Mlle de Lespinasse: Doctor, I see where you are getting and I bet. . . .

Bordeu: I never bet: you would win. Yes, Mademoiselle, that is my opinion.

Mlle de Lespinasse: And it makes no difference whether one keeps within the enclosure of one's own species or goes outside it.

Bordeu: Yes.

Mlle de Lespinasse: You are a monster.

Bordeu: Not I, but either nature or society. Listen, Mademoiselle, I am not one to be imposed upon by words, and I explain myself all the more freely because I am above board and the purity of my morals makes me invulnerable. Two actions are equally confined to the realm of pleasure; they can afford pleasure only, nothing useful; but one of these actions gives pleasure only to the person who practises it: the other enables the pleasure to be shared with a similar person either male or female, for here neither sex nor even the use of sex is relevant. For which of these two actions will commonsense pronounce ?

Mlle de Lespinasse: These questions are too sublime for me.

Bordeu: Ha! ha! So after being a man for five minutes, you resume your mob-cap and petticoats and become a woman again. That's right. Well, well, you must be treated as such. . . . Here is a fact, we hear no more of Mme du Barry. . . . You see, everything is arranged. People thought the Court was going to be turned upside down. The master has behaved like a sensible man. *Omne tulit punctum.* He kept the woman he liked and the minister he found useful. But you are not listening. Where are you ?

Mlle de Lespinasse: At those combinations, which all seem to me contrary to nature.

Bordeu: Nothing which is can be against or outside nature. I make no exception even for voluntary chastity and continence, which would be the first crimes against nature if one could sin against nature, and the first of crimes against social laws in a country where actions were weighed in any other balance than that of fanaticism and prejudice.

Mlle de Lespinasse: I come back to your wretched syllogisms and I see no middle point. One must deny or admit everything. . . . But come, Doctor, the best and shortest way is to jump over the mess and return to my first question. What do you think of the mingling of species ?

Bordeu: There is no need to jump for that. We were there already. Is your question one of physics or of ethics ?

Mlle de Lespinasse: Physics, physics.

Bordeu: So much the better: the ethical question comes first and you settle it. And so . . .

Mlle de Lespinasse: Of course. Doubtless it is preliminary. But I should like you to . . . separate cause and effect. Leave the nasty cause on one side.

Bordeu: You are asking me to begin at the end. But as you wish it, I will tell you that, thanks to our cowardice, our inhibitions, our laws or prejudices, very few experiments have been made: we do not know what copulations would be quite sterile; in what cases the useful and the agreeable would be combined: what sort of species one could guarantee as a result of varied and consistent experiments: if fauns are real or fabulous: if one could not multiply the race of mules in a hundred different ways; if those of which we know are really sterile. But there is one curious fact, which is false, but which an infinity of persons will assure you to be true, that they have seen in the farmyard of the archduke a scoundrelly rabbit who played the part of a cock to a score of scoundrelly hens who raised no objection; they will add that they have been shown chickens covered with fur, the fruit of this bestiality. You can imagine how people laughed at them.

Mlle de Lespinasse: But what do you mean by consistently followed-up experiments ?

Bordeu: I mean that the circulation of creatures is gradual, and that their assimilation should be prepared in advance, and that, to succeed in these sorts of experiments, you must begin a long way off and first work to bring these animals nearer together by giving them a similar regime.

Mlle de Lespinasse: It will be difficult to get men to browse.

Bordeu: But not to get them to take goat's milk, and easy to get goats to eat bread. I have my private reasons for choosing goats.

Mlle de Lespinasse: And what are those reasons ?

Bordeu: You are very bold! Because—because we can breed from them a race which is vigorous, intelligent, indefatigable, and swift, which we can make into excellent servants.

Mlle de Lespinasse: Splendid, Doctor. I already seem to see behind the carriages of your duchesses five or six goat-foots. I like the idea.

Bordeu: And we should no longer degrade our brothers by subjecting them to functions unworthy of themselves and us.

Mlle de Lespinasse: Better and better.

Bordeu: And we should no longer reduce the human race in our colonies to the condition of beasts of burden.

Mlle de Lespinasse: Quick, Doctor, get to work, and make us these goat-foots.

Bordeu: And you have no scruples in allowing it ?

Mlle de Lespinasse: Stop, I have thought of one. Your goat-foots will be shocking rakes.

Bordeu: I cannot guarantee their morals.

Mlle de Lespinasse: There will be no security for chaste women: they will multiply endlessly: and eventually we shall have to crush them or obey them. I no longer want them. I no longer want them. You had better keep quiet.

Bordeu: And the question of their baptism?

Mlle de Lespinasse: Would be a fine kettle of fish for the Sorbonne.

Bordeu: Have you seen, at the Zoo, in a glass cage, an ourang-outang with the look of St John preaching in the desert?

Mlle de Lespinasse: Yes, I have.

Bordeu (*going away*): The Cardinal de Polignac said to it one day: "Speak, and I baptize thee."

Mlle de Lespinasse: Good-bye, then, Doctor: don't abandon us for centuries, as is your custom, and sometimes think how I love you to madness. Suppose people knew of all the horrors you have been telling me?

Bordeu: I am quite certain you will keep quiet about it.

Mlle de Lespinasse: Do not be too confident! I listen only for the pleasure of repeating. But one word more and I never return to the subject again.

Bordeu: What is it?

Mlle de Lespinasse: All these abominable tendencies, what do they arise from?

Bordeu: Everywhere from a poverty of organism in young people and a corruption of the brain in old ones: from the love of beauty in Athens: from the shortage of women in Rome: from fear of the pox in Paris. Good-bye, good-bye!

SUPPLEMENT TO THE VOYAGE OF BOUGAINVILLE

I

Judgment on the Voyage of Bougainville

A.: That superb starry vault, under which we came back yesterday, and which seemed to promise a fine day, has not kept its word.

B.: And what do you know about it ?

A.: The fog is so thick that it forbids us even the sight of the neighbouring trees.

B.: True. But suppose this fog, which only remains in the lower part of the atmosphere because it is considerably charged with damp, falls back on the earth ?

A.: And suppose on the contrary it traverses the sponge, gains the upper region where the air is thinner, and (as the chemists say) resists saturation.

B.: We must wait and see.

A.: And what are you doing while you wait ?

B.: Reading.

A.: Always that voyage of Bougainville ?

B.: Yes.

A.: I do not understand the man at all. The study of mathematics, which presupposes a sedentary life, filled his early years. Now he passes suddenly from a life of meditation and retirement to the active, painful, wandering and distracted profession of a traveller.

B.: Not at all. His vessel is only a floating house. After all, the navigator travels enormous distances, shut up and motionless in quite a narrow space. He makes the tour of the globe on a plank as you and I make the tour of the universe on your floor.

A.: There is another apparent subject for surprise, the contradiction between the character of the man and his undertaking. Bougainville is fond of the amusements society can offer. He likes women, theatres, good food. He gives himself over to the whirl of the world, with as good grace as to the inconstancy of the elements upon which he has been tossed. He is good-natured and light-hearted; a typical Frenchman, ballasted on one side with a treatise of differential and integral calculus, and on the other with a voyage round the globe.

B.: He is like everybody else. He distracts himself after concentration and concentrates after distraction.

A.: And what do you think of his Voyage?

B.: As far as I can judge from a quite superficial reading, I should say it was specially helpful in three ways. It affords us a better knowledge of our old home and its inhabitants; greater security on the seas he traversed sounding-lead in hand, and greater accuracy in our geographical charts. Bougainville started with the necessary knowledge, and the qualities suitable to that knowledge: philosophy, courage, truth, a power of rapid summing-up, which seizes on things and shortens the necessary period of observation: circumspection, patience; the desire to see, to clear his mind, to be instructed, knowledge of the calculus, mechanics, geometry, astronomy, and an adequate tincture of natural history.

A.: And what about his style?

B.: No nonsense about it. The tone of the thing is simplicity and clearness, especially when one is familiar with the language of sailors.

A.: Was his journey a long one?

B.: I have traced it on this globe. You see this line of red points?

A.: Which starts from Nantes?

B.: Yes, and runs to the Straits of Magellan, enters the Pacific, winds between the islands forming that immense archipelago which stretches from the Philippines to New Holland, skirts Madagascar and the Cape of Good Hope, continues into the Atlantic, follows the coast of Africa, and joins up one of its extremities to that from which the navigator embarked.

A.: He suffered a deal of hardship.

B.: Every navigator exposes himself, and willingly, to peril of air, fire, earth and water. But that after having wandered months together between sea and heaven, death and life: after being struck by tempests, threatened with death by wreck, illness, shortage of food and water, a poor wretch should arrive with his ship smashed, and fall expiring with fatigue and misery at the feet of a brazen monster who refuses him the most urgent remedies or mercilessly makes him wait, that indeed is hard.

A.: It is a crime that ought to be punished.

B.: One of those calamities on which the traveller has not counted.

A.: And should not have to count. I thought the European powers sent to govern their possessions overseas only honourable natures, benevolent men, souls filled with humanity and capable of sympathy.

B.: That is the last thing they care about!

A.: There are some curious things in this Voyage of Bougainville?

B.: Plenty.

A.: Does he not assert that wild animals come up to men, and birds come to settle on them, before they have learned the danger that springs from such familiarity?

B.: Others have said that before him.

A.: How does he explain the fact that some animals inhabit islands separated from the mainland by terrifying stretches of sea? Who brought the wolf there, or the fox, the dog, the stag, the snake?

B.: He explains nothing. He merely states the fact.

A. And you, how do you explain it?

B.: Who knows the first history of our globe? How many stretches of land, now isolated, were once joined up? The only phenomenon about which one could form some conjecture is the direction taken by the mass of waters which has separated them.

A.: And how so?

B.: From the general lines followed by the erosion. Some day we will amuse ourselves with this study, if you care to. And now, look at that island called The Lancers.* Everyone who observes its position on the globe wonders who placed men there: what ties formally bound them to the rest of their species: what happens to them as they multiply on an area not more than two miles in diameter.

A.: They kill and eat each other. And here, perhaps, we see a first period of cannibalism which would be very ancient and quite natural, insular in origin.

B.: Or multiplication of the species is limited by some superstitious law: there the infant is crushed in the body of its mother, who is trampled under foot by a priestess.

A.: Or the man expires with his throat cut, under the knife of the priest: or men have recourse to the castration of males.

B.: And the infibulation of females. From this springs many a custom of a strange inevitable cruelty,

* Also called Akiaki, a tiny island in the Low Archipelago, N.E. from New Zealand.

of which the cause is lost in the night of time and becomes a matter of torture to philosophers. One thing has been consistently observed. Supernatural and divine institutions strengthen themselves and become eternal, by becoming transformed in the long run into civil and national laws, while civil and national institutions become consecrated, and degenerate into supernatural and divine precepts.

A. That is one of the gloomiest of all vicious circles.

B.: One strand the more to add to the cord that binds us.

A.: Was he not in Paraguay just at the moment when the Jesuits were expelled ?

B.: Yes.

A.: What does he say about it ?

B.: Less than he might. But enough to tell me that these cruel Spartans in the black jacket used their Indian slaves as the Lacedemonians did their helots: condemned them to continual toil: made them drink their own sweat; and allowed them no right of property: kept them in degraded superstition; exacted from them profound veneration: strode among them whip in hand, and struck without distinction of age or sex. A hundred years more and their expulsion would have been impossible or entailed a long war between the monks and their sovereign, whose authority they had bit by bit thrown off.

A.: And those Patagonians about whom Doctor Maby and La Condamine of the Academy have made such a to-do ?

B.: Very good fellows who come up and hug you, crying Chaoua. Strong, vigorous, and yet rarely more than six foot high: with nothing gigantic about them, but their corpulence, the size of their heads, and the thickness of their limbs. Man is born with love for the marvellous and exaggerates everything round him. How should he then keep his sense of proportion about things, when he has, so to speak, to justify his journey and the trouble he has taken in going so far to see them?

A.: And what does he think of the savage?

B.: Apparently the cruel character sometimes observed in him is due to his daily war of defence against the animal creation. He is always innocent and gentle where nothing troubles his repose and security. All wars originate in a common claim to the same piece of property. Civilized man has a common claim along with another civilized man to the possession of a field, where they already occupy the two ends. And this field becomes a subject of dispute between them.

A.: And the tiger has a common claim, along with the savage man, to the possession of a forest. This is the first claim and the cause of the earliest of wars. Have you seen the Tahitien whom Bougainville took on board and brought back here?

B.: Yes. He was called Aotourou. He took the first piece of land he saw for the home of the travellers. Either they had lied to him about the length of the journey, or else he was deceived quite naturally by the apparently small distance between the shores of the sea, by which he dwelt, to the spot where the sky seemed to merge in the horizon, and knew nothing about the real measurement of the earth. The holding of women in common was a custom so well established in his mind that he threw himself on the first European woman he met, and very seriously intended to show her the courtesy of Tahiti. He grew bored with us. As the Tahitien alphabet has neither b, c, d, f, g, x, y nor z, he could never learn to speak our language. It offered his rigid organs too many strange articulations and new sounds. He never stopped sighing after his own country, and I am not surprised at it. The voyage of

Bougainville is the only one to give me the taste for a country other than my own. Till I had read it, I had always thought that one was nowhere so contented as at home; a state of mind which held good, I thought, for each inhabitant of the globe; and which sprang quite naturally from the charm of the soil, and the comforts which gather round the conveniences one enjoys and is not equally sure of finding elsewhere.

A.: What! Do you not think that the inhabitants of Paris are as sure that corn grows in the Roman Campagna as in the fields of the Beauce?

B.: No, I do not. Bougainville sent back Aotourou, after providing for his expenses and the safety of his journey.

A.: O Aotourou! How happy wilt thou be to see once more thy father, thy mother, thy brothers, thy sisters, thy mistresses, thy compatriots! What wilt thou tell them of us?

B.: Very little, and that they will not believe.

A.: Why very little?

B.: Because he has taken in very little, and because he will find in his own language no terms corresponding to that little of which he has gathered some notion.

A.: And why will they not believe him?

B.: Because after comparing their own customs to ours, they will rather think Aotourou a liar than believe we are so mad.

A.: Really?

B.: No doubt of it. Savage life is so simple and our societies are such complicated mechanisms. The Tahitien is near the origin of the world, the European near its old age. The interval which separates him and us is greater than that between the child at birth and the tottering old man. He understands nothing of our laws and customs or only sees in them impediments disguised in a hundred forms, impediments which can excite only the indignation and contempt of a being in whom the sentiment of liberty is the deepest of all.

A.: Do you want to weave a fable round Tahiti?

B.: This is no fable: and you would have no doubt as to the sincerity of Bougainville if you knew the supplement to his voyage.

A.: And where is this supplement to be found?

B.: There, on that table.

A.: Will you trust me with it?

B.: No. But we can run through it together if you like.

A.: Certainly, I like. See, the fog is falling again and the blue of the sky is beginning to appear. It seems my fate to be in the wrong with you about the smallest things. I must be very good-natured to overlook such an unfailing superiority as yours.

B. Come, come, read. Skip the preamble, which is unimportant, and go straight on to the farewell addressed by the chief of the island to our travellers. That will give you some idea of these people's eloquence.

A.: How did Bougainville understand these farewells pronounced in a language he did not know?

B.: You will see. It is an old man talking.

II

The Old Man's Farewell

He was the father of a large family. On the arrival of the Europeans, he cast looks of disdain at them, showing neither astonishment, fright, nor curiosity.*

* The presence of this old man and his attitude to the Europeans are mentioned by Bougainville.

They came up to him: he turned his back on them and retired into his cabin. His silence and his anxiety revealed his thoughts too well. He groaned within himself over the happy days of his country, now for ever eclipsed. On the departure of Bougainville, as the inhabitants rushed in a crowd on to the beach, attached themselves to his clothing, hugged his comrades in their arms and wept, this old man advanced, severe in mien, and said: "Weep, luckless Tahitiens, weep, but for the arrival not for the departure of these ambitious and wicked men. One day you will know them better. One day they will return, holding in one hand the morsel of wood you see attached to this man's belt, in the other, the iron which hangs from that man's side: they will return to throw you into chains, to cut your throats, or to subject you to their extravagance and vices: one day you will serve under them, as corrupted, as vile, as luckless as they. One consolation I have. My life is drawing to its close. And the calamity I announce to you, I shall not see. O Tahitiens, my friends, there is one method which might save you from your tragic future. But I would rather die than advise it. Let them withdraw and live."

Then addressing Bougainville, he added:

"And thou, chief of the brigands who obey thee, quickly push off thy vessel from our shore. We are innocent; we are happy: and thou canst not but spoil our happiness. We follow the pure instinct of nature: thou hast sought to efface its character from our souls. Here all things belong to all men. Thou hast preached some strange distinction between 'thine' and 'mine.' Our daughters and our wives were held in common by us all: thou hast shared this privilege with us, and thou hast come and inflamed them with frenzies unknown before. They have lost their reason in thy arms. Thou hast become ferocious in theirs. They have come to hate each other. You have slaughtered each other for them: they have come back stained with your blood. We are free: and see thou hast planted in our earth the title of our future slavery. Thou art neither god nor demon. Who art thou then to make slaves? Orou! thou who understandest the language of these men, tell us all as thou hast told me, what they have written on this metal blade! *This country is ours.* This country is thine! And why? Because thou hast set foot there? If a Tahitien disembarked one day upon your shores, and graved upon one of your stones or on the bark of one of your trees: *This country belongs to the inhabitants of Tahiti*, what wouldst thou think of such a proceeding? Thou art the stronger! But what of that? When someone took from you one of those rubbishy trifles with which your hut is filled, thou didst cry out and take thy revenge. Yet at that moment thou wast projecting in the depth of thy heart the theft of a whole country. Thou art not a slave. Thou wouldst suffer death rather than become one, yet us thou wouldst enslave. Thinkest thou then that the Tahitien cannot defend his liberty and die? He, whom thou wishest to seize like an animal, the Tahitien, is thy brother. You are both children of nature. What right hast thou over him that he has not over thee? Thou art come. Did we fall upon thee? Did we pillage thy ship? Did we seize thee and expose thee to the arrows of our enemies? Did we yoke thee to our animals toiling in the fields? No. We have respected our image in thee. Leave us our customs. They are wiser and more honourable than thine. We have no wish to barter what thou callest our ignorance against thy useless knowledge. We possess all that is necessary and good for us. Do we deserve contempt because we have not known how to fabricate for ourselves wants in superfluity? When we are hungry we have enough to eat; when we are cold, the means to clothe ourselves. Thou hast entered our cabins. What, in thy opinion, is lacking? Pursue as long as thou wilt what thou callest the commodities of life. But permit sensible beings to stop, when by continuing their painful labour they will gain but imaginary good. If thou persuadest us to cross the narrow limit of necessity, when shall we stop working? What time will be left over for enjoying ourselves? We have reduced to the smallest possible the sum of our annual and daily toil, because to us nothing seems better than repose. Go back to thine own country to trouble and torment thyself as much as thou wilt. Trouble us neither with thy artificial needs, nor thy imaginary virtues. Look at these men: how straight, healthy, and robust they are! Look at these women! How straight, healthy, fresh and fair they are. Take this bow. It is mine. Call to help thee, one, two, three, four of thy comrades and try to bend it. I bend it myself alone. I plough the earth. I climb the mountain. I pierce the forest. I cover a league of the plain in less than an hour. Thy young companions can scarcely follow me, and I am ninety years old and more. Woe to this island! Woe to all Tahitiens present and to come for the day of this thy visit! We only know one illness that to which man, animal and plant have been condemned, old age: and thou hast brought to us another. Thou hast infected our blood. Perhaps we shall have to exterminate with our own hands, our daughters, our wives, our children: the men who have approached thy women: the women who have approached thy men. Our fields will be damp with the impure blood which has passed from thy veins into ours: else our children will be condemned to nourish and perpetuate the ill thou hast given to their fathers and mothers and to transmit it for ever to their descendants. Wretch! thou wilt be guilty of the ravages that follow thy fatal embraces or of the murders we shall commit to check the poison! Thou speakest of crimes! Knowest thou a greater than thine own? What with thee is the punishment for the man who kills his neighbour? Death by iron. And what for the coward who poisons him? Death by fire. Compare thy crime to this latter one, and tell us, poisoner of nations, the punishment thou deservest. A moment ago the young Tahitien maiden abandoned herself with transport to the embraces of the Tahitien boy: she waited with impatience till her mother (authorized by her reaching the nubile age), raised her veil and bared her throat. She was proud to excite the desires or to fix the amorous gaze of the stranger, her parents or her brother. She accepted fearlessly and shamelessly, in our presence, midst a circle of innocent Tahitiens, to the sound of flutes, between the dances, the caresses of him her young heart and the secret voice of her senses had chosen. The idea of crime and the danger of disease have come with thee amongst us. Our pleasures, formerly so sweet, are accompanied by remorse and terror. That man in black, next you, who listens to me, has spoken to our boys. I know not what he has said to our girls. But our boys hesitate: our girls blush. Plunge if thou wilt into the dark forest with the perverse partner of thy pleasures, but allow the good and simple Tahitiens to reproduce without shame, in the face of heaven and the open day. What sentiment more honourable and greater couldst thou find to replace the one we have breathed into them and which animates their lives? They think the moment has come to enrich the nation and the family with a new citizen and they glory in it. They eat to live and to grow. They grow to multiply, they find there neither vice nor shame. Listen to the succession of thy crimes. Scarcely hast thou appeared among them, but they turn thieves. Scarcely hadst thou descended on our soil, but it smoked blood. That Tahitien who ran to meet thee, who greeted thee, who received thee crying *Taïo, friend, friend:* you killed him. And why did you kill him? Because he had been seduced by the glitter of thy little serpents' eggs. He gave thee his fruits: he offered thee his wife and daughter: he yielded thee his cabin. And thou hast killed him for a handful of these grains, which he took from thee without asking. And this people? At the sound of thy deadly firearms, terror seized them and they fled into the mountain. But understand they would have speedily come down again. Without me you may be sure you would all have perished in an instant. Why have I calmed, why have I restrained them? Why do I restrain them even now? I do not know. For thou deservest no sentiment of pity. Thou hast a ferocious soul which never felt it. Thou didst walk, thou and thine, in our island: thou hast been respected: thou hast enjoyed everything: thou hast found in thy way neither barrier nor refusal: thou wast invited in: thou sattest down: there was laid out before thee the abundance of the country. Didst thou wish for our young girls? Save for these, who have not yet the privilege of showing face and throat, their mothers presented thee them all quite naked. Thine the tender victim of hostly duty. For her and for thee the ground hast been scattered with leaves and flowers: the musicians have tuned their instruments: nothing has troubled the sweetness nor hindered the liberty of her caresses or thine. The hymn was chanted, the hymn which exhorted thee to be a man and our child to be a woman, a woman yielding and voluptuous. There was dancing round your bed, and it is on leaving the arms of this woman, after feeling on her breast the sweetest rapture, that thou hast killed her brother, her friend, her father perhaps. Thou hast done worse still. Look this way. See this enclosure stiff with arms: these arms which had only menaced our enemies, they are turned against our own children: see the wretched companions of our pleasures: see their sadness. See the grief of their fathers: the despair of their mothers. In that place they have been condemned to perish by our hands or by the ills that thou hast done them. Withdraw unless thy cruel eyes take pleasure in spectacles of death: withdraw, go, and may the guilty seas which have spared thee in thy voyage gain their own absolution and avenge us by swallowing thee up before thy return. And you, Tahitiens, return to your cabins every one of you and let these unworthy strangers hear on their departure but the moaning wave, and see but the foam whose fury whitens a deserted beach."

He had scarcely finished, but the crowd of inhabitants had disappeared. A vast silence reigned over all the island. Nothing was heard but the shrill whistle of the winds and the dull noise of the water along all the coast. One might have thought that air and water, responsive to the old man's voice, were happy to obey him.

Well, what do you think of it?

A.: A vehement discourse. But for all its somewhat abrupt and savage style I seem to detect in it European ideas and turns of speech.

B.: You must realize that it is translated from Tahitien into Spanish, and from Spanish into French. The old man had gone at night to this Orou, whom he questioned and in whose hut the use of the Spanish tongue had been preserved from time immemorial. Orou had written out the old man's speech in Spanish; and Bougainville had a copy of it in his hand, while the Tahitien spoke it.

A.: So far I see only too well why Bougainville suppressed this fragment. But that is not everything, and I am very curious about the rest.

B.: The sequel will not interest you so much perhaps.

A.: No matter.

B.: It is a conversation between the ship's chaplain and a native of the island.

A.: Orou?

B.: The same. When Bougainville's vessel approached Tahiti, an infinite number of hollowed trees were thrown on the water. In a moment his ship was surrounded by them. Wherever he looked, he perceived demonstrations of surprise and kindness. Food was thrown and arms extended to him. Men attached themselves by cords and climbed up the planks. His launch was full of them. They cried towards the beach and their cries were answered. The natives of the island came running up. Now everyone is on shore. They seize the crew and divide them out. Each took his own choice into his hut. The men hugged them by the waist: the women stroked their cheeks with their hands. Put yourself in the crew's position. Witness with your mind's eye this scene of hospitality and give me your opinion of the human race.

A.: A delightful one.

B.: I nearly forgot to mention a curious incident. This scene of benevolence and humanity was suddenly interrupted by the cries of a man calling out for help, the servant of one of Bougainville's officers. Some young Tahitiens had thrown themselves at him, stretched him on the ground, taken his clothes off, and were preparing to show him the final courtesy.

A.: What! these simple people, these good worthy savages?

B.: You are quite wrong. This servant was a woman disguised as a man, a fact that was never discovered by a single member of the crew during the whole period of their long voyage. But the Tahitiens divined her sex at the first glance. She came from Burgundy and was called Barré, neither pretty nor ugly, and twenty-six years old. She had never left her village and her first notion of a journey was to go round the world. She always showed good sense and courage.

A.: These slender mechanisms sometimes encase very strong souls.

III

Conversation of the Chaplain and Orou

B.: In the division which the Tahitiens made of Bougainville's crew, the chaplain fell to the lot of Orou. They were about the same age, thirty-five to thirty-six. Just then Orou had at home only his wife and three daughters, Asto, Palli and Thia. These undressed him, washed his face, hands and feet, and served him a healthy and frugal meal. When he was about to go to bed, Orou, who had gone away with his family, reappeared, presented his wife and three daughters quite naked and said:

"Thou hast had supper, thou art young and in good health. Sleep alone, and thou wilt sleep badly. Man needs a companion by his side at night. Here is my wife, here are my daughters. Take your choice. But you would oblige me by fixing for preference on my youngest daughter, who has not yet had a child."

The mother added: "Alas! Alas! But it is no good complaining. Poor Thia, it is not her fault."

The chaplain replied that his religion, his calling, good morals and honourability forbade him to accept these offers.

Orou replied: "I do not know what thou meanest by religion, but I cannot think well of it, if it forbids thee to enjoy an innocent pleasure, to which nature, the sovereign mistress, invites us all—to give existence to one like thee: to render a service that father, mother and children ask of thee; to make a fitting return to a host who has welcomed thee warmly and to enrich a nation, by increase, with one subject the more. I do not know what thou meanest by thy calling. But thy first duty is to be a man and grateful. I dare not suggest that thou carry away into thy country the morals of Orou. But Orou, thy host and friend, beseeches thee to lend thyself to the morals of Tahiti. Are the morals of Tahiti better or worse than yours? It is a question that can be easily settled. Has the country of thy birth more children than it can feed? In that case thy morals are neither better nor worse than ours. Can it feed more than it has? Then our morals are better than thine. As for the honourability thou objectest against me, I understand thee. I admit my fault and hope to be forgiven. I do not ask thee to damage thy health. If thou art tired, thou must rest. But I hope thou wilt not continue to sadden us. See the care thou hast spread on all these faces. They fear thou hast remarked in them some faults which have made thee disdain them. But even so, would not the pleasure of honouring one of my daughters, among her companions and sisters, and doing a good action, make up for this? Be generous."

THE CHAPLAIN: It is not that: they are all four equally beautiful: but my religion! but my calling!

OROU: They belong to me and I offer them to thee. They are their own and they give themselves to thee. Whatever may be the purity of conscience which the thing *religion* and the thing *calling* prescribe, thou canst accept them without scruple. I do not abuse my authority; thou mayest be certain I know and respect the rights of men.

Here the candid chaplain admits that never had Providence enforced him to so formidable a temptation.

He was young: he was excited: he was tormented. He diverted his eyes from the charming suppliants: but always brought them back again. He raised his hands and his eyes to heaven. Thia, the youngest, embraced his knees, and said:

"Stranger, afflict not my father, afflict not my mother; afflict not me. Honour me in the hut and among my people. Raise me to the rank of my sisters, who laugh at me. Asto, the eldest, has three children already, Palli, the second, two, and Thia none at all. Stranger, honest stranger, do not rebuff me: make me a mother: give me a child whom one day I may lead by the hand, beside me, in Tahiti; who may be seen, in nine months' time, hanging from my breast: one of whom I may be proud and take with me as part of my dowry, when I pass from my father's cabin to another's. Perhaps I shall have more luck with thee than with our young Tahitiens. Grant me this favour and I will never forget thee: I will bless thee all my life. I will write thy name on my arm and on that of thy son. We will pronounce it unceasingly with joy. And when thou shalt quit this shore, my wishes shall go along with thee over the sea, till thou art arrived in thine own country."

The frank chaplain adds that she clasped his hands and gazed on him with the most touching and expressive looks: that she wept: that her father, mother, and sisters withdrew: that he remained alone with her and after repeating "But my religion, but my calling" he found himself next day lying beside this girl, who overwhelmed him with caresses and invited father, mother, and sisters, when they approached the bed, to join their gratitude to hers. Asto and Palli, who had gone away, returned with the food of the country, drink and fruit. They embraced their sister and offered up their vows for her. They breakfasted together and then Orou, who remained alone with the chaplain, said:

"I see my daughter is well satisfied with thee and I thank thee. But pray tell me what is this word religion, that thou didst repeat so often and with so much pain?"

The chaplain, after reflecting for a moment, answered: "Who made thy cabin and its articles of furniture?"

Orou: I did.

Chaplain: Very well. We believe that this world and all it contains is the work of a workman.

Orou: Then he has feet, hands and a head?

Chaplain: No.

Orou: Where does he live?

Chaplain: Everywhere.

Orou: Here too?

Chaplain: Yes.

Orou: We have never seen him.

Chaplain: He is not to be seen.

Orou: A poor sort of father! He must be old. For he must be at least as old as his handiwork.

Chaplain: He never grows old. He has spoken to our ancestors: he has given them laws: and has prescribed the manner in which he would be honoured. He has ordained for them certain actions as good and forbidden them others as bad.

Orou: I see, and one of those actions he has forbidden as bad is to sleep with a woman or girl. Why then has he made two sexes?

Chaplain: For union, but on certain fixed conditions, and after certain preliminary ceremonies, as a result of which a man belongs to a woman and belongs to her alone. A woman belongs to a man and belongs to a man alone.

Orou: For their whole life?

CHAPLAIN: For their whole life.

OROU: So that if a woman slept with anyone else than her husband and a husband with anyone else than his wife—but the case can never arise, for since the workman is there and disapproves of it, he knows how to stop them.

CHAPLAIN: No, he lets them go their way, and they sin against the law of God (for that is what we call the great workman) and the law of the land; and they commit a crime.

OROU: I should hate to offend you with my remarks, but with your permission, I will give you my opinion.

CHAPLAIN: Go on.

OROU: I find these singular precepts opposed to nature and contrary to reason: they needs must multiply the number of crimes and continually annoy the old workman, who has made everything without the help of head, hands, or tools, who exists everywhere and is to be seen nowhere: who endures to-day and to-morrow and is never a day the older: who commands and is never obeyed: who can prevent and does not do so. These precepts are contrary to nature because they presuppose that a thinking, feeling, free being can be the property of another like himself. Upon what can this right be founded? Do you not see that, in your country, you have mixed up two different things? That which has neither feeling, thought, desire nor will, and which one can take, keep or exchange, without its suffering or complaining; and that which cannot be exchanged or acquired: which has liberty, will, desires: which can give itself and refuse itself for a single instant, or for ever: which complains and suffers: which could not become a mere article of commerce without its character being forgotten and violence done to its nature? These precepts are contrary to the general law of existence. Does anything really appear to thee more senseless than a precept which refuses to admit the change which is in ourselves: which insists on a constancy which has no counterpart in us and which violates the liberty of male and female, by chaining them for ever one to the other: more senseless than a constancy which confines the most capricious of pleasures to a single person: than an oath of immutability between two fleshly beings in the face of a heaven which is not a moment the same: under caverns that threaten ruin: beneath a rock that falls in powder: at the foot of a tree that cracks: upon a stone that breaks in pieces? Believe me, you have made the condition of men worse than that of animals. I know not who thy great workman is. But I am glad he has never spoken to our fathers and I hope he never speaks to our children. For he might say the same silly things to them and they might be silly enough to believe him. Yesterday at supper thou toldest of *magistrates* and *priests*, whose authority rules your conduct. But tell me, are they lords of good and evil? Can they make what is just unjust, and what is unjust just? Does it rest with them to label good actions harmful and harmful actions innocent or useful? Thou canst not well admit it, for then there would be neither true nor false, good nor bad, beautiful nor ugly, except in so far as thy great workman, thy magistrates and priests thought good to say so. Then from one moment to another thou wouldst be compelled to change thy opinion and thy conduct. One day one of thy three masters would give the order *kill* and thou wouldst be obliged, in conscience, to kill. Another day *steal* and thou wouldst have to steal; or, *Do not eat this fruit* and thou wouldst not dare eat it; or, *I forbid thee this fruit or animal* and thou couldst not touch it. There is no goodness they could not forbid thee: no wickedness they could not order. And where wouldst thou be, if thy three masters, falling out among themselves, took it into their heads to permit, enjoin and forbid the same thing as I am sure often happens? Then to please the priest, thou must needs quarrel with the magistrate: to satisfy the magistrate, thou must anger the great workman; and to be agreeable to the great workman, turn thy back on nature. Knowest thou what will happen? Thou willst get to despise all three! be neither man, citizen, nor pious person: thou wilt be nothing: on bad terms with all sorts of authority and with thyself: wicked, tormented in heart: persecuted by thy insensate masters: and wretched as I saw thee yesterday evening when I presented my wife and daughters to thee and thou didst cry out: "But my religion, but my calling." Dost thou wish to know what is good and bad in all times and all places? Cling to the nature of things and actions: to thy relations with those like thee: to the influence of thy conduct on thy private convenience and the public good. Thou art mad if thou thinkest there be anything, high or low, in the universe which can supplement or be subtracted from the law of nature. Her eternal will is that good be preferred to evil and public to private good. Thou mayest aver the opposite but thou wilt not be obeyed. Thou wilt multiply the number of malefactors and those made wretched by fear, punishment or remorse. Thou wilt deprave men's consciences and corrupt their minds. They will no longer know what to do or what to avoid. Troubled in their state of innocence, calm in sin, they will have lost their pole-star on their journey. Answer me frankly. In spite of the express order of thy three legislators, does a young man in your country never sleep with a girl without their permission?

CHAPLAIN: I should lie, if I asserted it.

OROU: And does the woman, who has sworn to belong only to her husband, never give herself to another?

CHAPLAIN: Nothing is commoner.

OROU: In these cases thy legislators either do or do not take action. If they do, they are wild beasts who make war on nature. If not, they are imbeciles, who have exposed their authority to contempt by a useless prohibition.

CHAPLAIN: The guilty ones, when they escape the severity of the law, are chastised by public disapproval.

OROU: You mean that justice functions through the absence of common sense in a whole nation: that a maniacal public opinion does duty for the laws.

CHAPLAIN: The girl who has been dishonoured can no longer find a husband.

OROU: Dishonoured! Why?

CHAPLAIN: The faithless wife is more or less despised.

OROU: Despised! Why?

CHAPLAIN: The young man is called a cowardly seducer.

OROU: Cowardly! A seducer! Why?

CHAPLAIN: Father, mother and children are heart-broken: the flighty husband is a libertine: the betrayed husband shares his wife's disgrace.

OROU: What a monstrous tissue of extravagances are you detailing to me! And even now thou hast not yet told me everything. For the moment men are allowed to regulate at will notions of justice and property, to endow things with some particular character or deprive them of it arbitrarily, to associate good and bad with certain actions or the reverse, then, by consulting only their own caprice, the men become censorious, vindictive, suspicious, tyrannical, envious, jealous, deceitful, uncomfortable, secretive, dissimulating. They spy, they cheat, they quarrel, they lie. Daughters impose on their parents, husbands on their wives, wives on their husbands. Girls, yes, I am sure of it girls will suffocate their children: suspicious parents will despise and neglect theirs; mothers will abandon them to the mercy of fate: crime and debauchery will appear in all their forms. I know it all, as well as if I had lived among you. It is so, because it cannot be otherwise: and thy society, which your chief praises for its order, turns out to be only a collection of hypocrites, who secretly stamp the laws under foot: or unfortunates who are themselves the instruments of their own torture by submitting to such laws: or imbeciles in whom prejudice has completely stifled the law of nature: or beings of feeble organism, in whom nature does not claim her rights.

CHAPLAIN: There is a resemblance certainly. So you have no marriage then?

OROU: Yes, we marry.

CHAPLAIN: What is marriage with you?

OROU: Agreement to share the same hut and sleep in the same bed as long as we wish to do so.

CHAPLAIN: And when you wish to no longer?

OROU: We separate.

CHAPLAIN: And what happens to the children?

OROU: Ah, stranger! Thy last question finally reveals to me the profound misery of thy country. Know, my friend, that here the birth of a child is always a source of happiness and its death a subject for regrets and tears. A child is a precious possession because it will become a man. So our care for them is quite different from our care for our plants and animals. The birth of a child is the occasion of domestic and public joy. It means an increase of fortune for the cabin and of strength for the nation, arms and hands the more in Tahiti. We see in him a farmer, a fisherman, a hunter, a soldier, a husband, a father. When a wife passes back from the cabin of her husband to that of her parents, she brings with her the children she had taken as a dowry: a division is made of those born during cohabitation: and as far as possible we share out the males and females so that each one may have about the same number of boys and girls.

CHAPLAIN: But children are for a long time a source of expense before doing any service in return.

OROU: We put aside for their upkeep and as provision for old people one-sixth of all the country's fruits. This tribute follows them everywhere. So you see a Tahitien family becomes richer the larger it grows.

CHAPLAIN: A sixth part!

OROU: Yes. It is a sure way of increasing the population and of interesting it in the respect due to old age and the rearing of children.

CHAPLAIN: Do your married couples sometimes take each other back again?

OROU: Very often. Meanwhile the shortest period of a marriage is from one moon to another.

CHAPLAIN: Unless the woman is with child; then cohabitation lasts at least nine months.

OROU: Thou art mistaken. Paternity like the tribute follows the child everywhere.

CHAPLAIN: Thou hast told me that a woman brings her children as a dowry to her husband?

OROU: Certainly. Take my eldest child, who has three children: they walk: they are healthy: they are handsome: they promise to be strong: when she takes it into her head to marry, she will take them with her; they are hers: her husband will receive them joyfully; and he would be all the more pleased with his wife were she about to have a fourth.

CHAPLAIN: By himself, I presume.

OROU: By himself or somebody else. The more children our daughters have, the more they are in demand. The robuster and stronger our boys are, the richer they are: and so we pay as much attention to preserving our girls from the approach of men and men from dealings with women before the fruitful age as to exhorting them to have children, when the boys have reached the age of puberty and the girls are nubile. You cannot imagine the importance of the service you will have rendered my daughter Thia if you have got her with child. Her mother will no longer say to her each month, "But Thia, what are you thinking about? You do not become pregnant. You are nineteen. You should have had two children already and you have not got any. Who is going to look after you? If you waste your youth like this, what will you do when you are old? Thia, you must have some fault that keep men away. Take yourself in hand, my child. By your age I had had three children."

CHAPLAIN: What steps do you take for looking after your sons and daughters during adolescence?

OROU: That is the chief object of domestic education and the most important point of public morals. Our boys, until the age of twenty-two, two or three years after the age of puberty, remain covered with a long tunic, their waist encircled by a small chain. Before they are nubile, our girls would never dare go out without a white veil.

Taking off the chain or raising the veil are faults rarely committed because our children are early taught the bad results that will ensue. But as soon as the male has reached his full strength, his symptoms of virility are continuous, and we are sure about the frequent effusion and the quality of the seminal fluid: the moment the girls become pale and listless, are sufficiently mature to conceive desires and to inspire and satisfy them usefully, the father removes the chain from his son, and cuts the nail of the middle finger of his right hand. The mother lifts up her daughter's veil. Now the one can solicit a woman and be solicited. The other can walk publicly with her face uncovered and her throat bare to accept or refuse a man's caresses. We merely indicate first to the boy the girl he should prefer and *vice versa*. In the case of a girl, the evening before, the young men assemble round the hut, and the air resounds all night with song and the noise of instruments. At daybreak she is led by her father and mother into an enclosure where there is dancing, displays of jumping, wrestling and racing. The male is exhibited naked before her, from every angle and in every attitude. In the case of boys, the girls pay them the honours and labour of the feast and expose to their regard the naked woman without reserve or secret. The rest of the ceremony finishes on a bed of leaves as thou sawest on thy arrival amongst us. At nightfall the girl returns to her parent's cabin or passes into the cabin of him she has chosen and remains there as long as she will.

CHAPLAIN: So this festival may or may not be a marriage-day?

OROU: Exactly.

A.: What is that I see there in the margin?

B.: It is a note in which the worthy chaplain says that the precepts of the parents on the choice of the boys and girls were full of very subtle and useful observations: but he has suppressed this part of the enquiry as it would have appeared unpardonably licentious to people as corrupt and superficial as ourselves. He added, however, that he regretted having had to cut down these details, as we might have observed from their study, first the point a nation, which concentrates in a single object, can reach in its researches, without the help of physics or anatomy, and secondly the differing ideas of beauty in people, who associate the human form with a moment's gratification and those who regard it rather from the aspect of utility and permanence. In Europe, in order to be beautiful, a woman must have a brilliant complexion, a broad forehead, large eyes, refined and delicate features, a slender waist, a small mouth, small hands, a small foot. Here practically none of these qualities are considered. The woman on whom glances fix and who is pursued by lovers is the one who holds out the promise of a large family (the woman of Cardinal D'Ossat), at once active, intelligent, brave, healthy and robust. There is practically nothing in common between the Venus of Athens and that of Tahiti. One is the gallant, the other the fruitful Venus. A Tahitien woman once said with contempt to another native—"You are beautiful, but your children are ugly. I am ugly, but my children are beautiful, and I am the one the men prefer."

After this note by the chaplain, Orou continues:

Orou: The happiest moment for a girl and her parents is when her pregnancy is remarked. She gets up: she runs around: she throws her arms round the neck of her mother and father: with transports of joy she announces and they learn the event. "Mamma, dear Papa. Kiss me! I am pregnant!" "Is it true?" "Quite true." "And by whom?" "By So and so."

Chaplain: How can she tell who the father is?

Orou: How not? Our loves last as long as our marriages. At the least from moon to moon.

Chaplain: And is this rule scrupulously observed?

Orou: You shall judge. First of all, the space of time between two moons is not a long one. But when two fathers have a well-founded claim to the paternity of a child, it does not belong to its mother any longer.

Chaplain: To whom does it belong then?

OROU: To the one of the two claimants she prefers. This is the beginning and the end of her privileges and a child being in itself an object of value and a source of wealth, thou wilt understand that with us loose women are rare and young men keep away from them.

CHAPLAIN: So you, too, have your loose women. I am glad to hear it.

OROU: We have even more than one kind: but you are taking me away from my subject. When one of our girls is with child, if the father is a handsome young man, well-built, brave, intelligent and hard-working, the hope that the child will inherit his father's virtues only adds to the general happiness. Our child is only ashamed if she has made a bad choice. Thou must understand the importance we attach to health, beauty, strength, industry, courage: thou must understand how, without our interference, the prerogatives of blood are forcibly perpetuated amongst us. Thou who hast journeyed in different countries, tell me, hast thou remarked in any of them as many handsome men or lovely women as in Tahiti? Look at me! What is thy opinion of me? Well, there are here ten thousand men taller and as strong, but not one braver than me: and so the mothers often indicate me to their daughters.

CHAPLAIN: But how many children come to thee of all those thou hast had outside thy cabin?

OROU: The fourth, be it male or female. We have established among ourselves a circulation of men, women and children, or rather arms of all ages and capacities, which is far more important than your merchandise, which is only the product of them.

CHAPLAIN: I understand. But what are those black veils I sometimes see?

OROU: The mask of barrenness, either a fault of birth or the consequence of advanced age. She who drops this veil and mingles with men is a loose woman, and the man who raises the veil and approaches a sterile woman is a libertine.

CHAPLAIN: Have you punishments for these libertines?

OROU: Only the punishment of disapproval.

CHAPLAIN: Can a father sleep with his daughter, a mother with her son, a brother with his sister, a husband with another man's wife?

OROU: Why not?

CHAPLAIN: We may tolerate fornication. But incest! But adultery!

OROU: What do you mean by these words *fornication, incest, adultery?*

CHAPLAIN: Crimes, terrible crimes, for any one of which men are burnt in my country.

OROU: I do not mind if people are burnt in thy country or not. But thou shalt not judge the morals of Europe by those of Tahiti nor those of Tahiti by thine own. We need a surer rule: and what shall that rule be? Do you know any other except the general good and private usefulness? Now tell me what there is contrary to our two ends of human action in thy crime *incest?* Thou art mistaken, my friend, if you thinkest all is said once a law is published, an ignominious word invented or a torture decreed. Answer me then, what meanest thou by incest?

CHAPLAIN: But an *incest* . . .

OROU: An *incest?* Is it so long ago that thy great workman without head, hands and tools made the world?

CHAPLAIN: No.

OROU: Did he make the whole human race at once?

CHAPLAIN: No, he only made a woman and a man.

Orou: Did they have children.

Chaplain: Certainly.

Orou: Suppose these two first parents had only had daughters, and their mother died the first, or that they only had sons, and the woman lost her husband.

Chaplain: That is a difficult question. But say what thou wilt, *incest* is an abominable crime. And now let us talk of something else.

Orou: Thou art pleased to say so. For myself, I express no opinion until thou tellest exactly what this abominable crime of incest is.

Chaplain: Very well. I admit that perhaps *incest* does not go against nature. But is not the fact that it is a menace to the political order sufficient? What would become of the safety of the chief and the tranquillity of the state if a whole nation composed of several million persons found itself revolving round fifty heads of families?

Orou: The worst that could happen would be that instead of one big society there would be fifty small ones, more happiness and one crime the less.

Chaplain: I suppose, however, that even here a son does not often sleep with his mother.

Orou: Not unless he has a great deal of respect for her, and a tenderness which makes him overlook difference of age and prefer a woman of forty to a girl of nineteen.

Chaplain: And the union of fathers and daughters?

Orou: Are hardly more common, unless the daughter be ugly and in small demand. If the father loves her, he sets to work to prepare her a dowry of children.

Chaplain: All this leads me to think that those whom nature has not favoured cannot be very happy in Tahiti.

Orou: Which shows thou hast no very high opinion of our young men's generosity.

Chaplain: As to the union of brother and sister. I suppose that is quite common.

Orou: And highly approved.

Chaplain: From what thou sayest, this passion, the source of so many crimes and ills in our country, must seem quite innocent to you.

Orou: Stranger, thou art without judgment and memory. Judgment, for whenever a thing is forbidden, one is naturally tempted to do it and one does it, and memory, for thou dost not remember what I told thee. We have dissolute old women who go out by night without their black veil and receive men when nothing can come of their connection. If they are recognized or caught they are punished with banishment to the north of the island as slaves: and we have precocious girls who remove their white veil without their parents' knowledge (and we have for them an enclosure in the hut): also we have young men who lay aside their chains before the time prescribed by nature and the law (and we reprimand their parents): we have women for whom the time of pregnancy is too long; unscrupulous women and girls who throw off their grey veils. But to tell the truth, we attach no great importance to any of these faults: thou canst have no notion how much the idea of private and public wealth, which is associated in our minds with the idea of population, purifies our morals in this matter.

Chaplain: But are not disorders occasioned by the passion of two men for the same woman or of two women or girls for the same man ?

Orou: I have not seen half a dozen examples. The man's or woman's choice finishes everything. Violence on the part of the man would be a serious fault. But a public complaint would be necessary, and it is almost unheard of for a woman or a girl to complain. All I have observed is that our women have less pity for ugly men than our young fellows for ill-favoured women. And that we do not mind.

CHAPLAIN: So I see you hardly know what jealousy is. But marital tenderness, motherly love, these two sentiments, so powerful and so sweet, must be fairly weak here if not quite unknown.

OROU: We have made up for them with another one, far more general, energetic and lasting, self-interest. Put thy hand upon thy conscience: leave out this fanfaronade of virtue which is for ever on the lips of thyself and thy comrades and which resides not in the bottom of their hearts. Tell me, if in any country in the world there exists a father, who save for the shame that restrains him, would not rather lose his son, a husband, who would not rather lose his wife than his fortune and his worldly comfort. And be sure that wherever man is attached to the preservation of one like him, as he is to his bed, his health, his repose, his cabin, his fruits, his fields, he will do his utmost for him. It is here that tears damp the couch of the suffering child; it is here that mothers are nursed in sickness: it is here that we prize a fruitful wife, a nubile daughter, an adolescent boy. It is here that we are busy with their establishment, because their preservation is always an increase, their loss a diminution of wealth.

CHAPLAIN: I am afraid this savage is right. The wretched peasant of our country, who overworks his wife to spare his horse, allows his children to perish without assisting them, and calls in the doctor for his ox.

OROU: I do not quite understand what thou hast just said: but on thy return to thy admirably regulated country, try to introduce this motive, and then people will appreciate the value of the child who is born and the importance of population. Wouldst thou have me reveal thee a secret? Let it go no further. You all arrive. We abandon you our wives and daughters: you are astonished. You show a gratitude that makes us laugh. You thank us when we are levying on thee and thy compatriots the heaviest of all impositions. We have not asked thee for money. We have not hurled ourselves on thy merchandise. We have despised thy goods. But our wives and daughters have come to squeeze out the blood from thy veins. When thou goest away, thou wilt have left us children behind thee. In thy opinion is not this tribute on thy person and on thy substance better than any other? If thou wouldst realise its worth, remember that thou hast two hundred leagues of coastline to traverse and that every twenty miles thou wilt be subject to the same tax. We have vast fields lying fallow. We have no arms to exploit them and we have asked thee for them. We have calamitous epidemics to make good and we have employed thee to repair the gaps they will leave. We have hostile neighbours to fight and need of soldiers; so we have asked thee to provide them. Our wives and daughters are too numerous for the men and we have associated thee in our task. Among our wives and daughters are some from whom we cannot breed and these we exposed first to your embraces. We have to pay a debt in men to a tyrannical neighbour: thou and thy comrades will meet the bill. And in five or six years we shall send them your sons, if they be not as good as ours. We are more robust and healthy than you; but we perceived you surpassed us in intelligence and immediately we decided that some of our fairest wives and daughters should gather in the seed of a race which is better than our own. It is an experiment we have made which may well be profitable. We have extracted from thee and thine the only advantage possible. And, believe me, savages as we are, we also know how to calculate. Go wherever thou wilt, and man will always be as subtle as thyself. He will never give thee anything save that which he does not want, and he will always ask for something useful from thee. If he gives thee a piece of gold for a piece of iron, it is that he cares nothing for gold and values iron. But now tell me why art thou not clothed like the others? What signifies that long cassock, which envelops thee from head to foot, and that pointed sack that thou lettest fall over thy shoulders or pullest over thy ears?

CHAPLAIN: The reason is, that such as I am, I am one of a society of men, called in my country monks. The most sacred of their vows is to have no dealings with women and not to have any children.

OROU: What do you do then?

CHAPLAIN: Nothing.

OROU: And thy magistrates tolerate this, the worst of all forms of idleness?

CHAPLAIN: More than that, they respect and make others respect it.

OROU: First, I had thought that nature, an accident or some cruel act had deprived you of the power to produce one in your image. And by pity, they preferred letting you live to killing you. But, monk, my daughter told me thou wert a man and a man as robust as any in Tahiti: further she had hopes thy repeated caresses would not be fruitless. Now that I understand why thou calledst out yesterday evening "*But my religion, but my calling,*" perhaps thou wilt tell me the reason for the favour and respect that the magistrates allow thee.

CHAPLAIN: I do not know.

OROU: But at least thou knowest why, being a man, thou hast willingly condemned thyself not to be one.

CHAPLAIN: That would be too long and difficult to explain.

Orou: And is the monk always faithful to this vow of barrenness?

Chaplain: No.

Orou: I was sure not. Have you also female monks?

Chaplain: Yes.

Orou: And are they as virtuous as the males?

Chaplain: They are more hedged in. They wither with grief and perish of boredom.

Orou: And so the injury done to nature is avenged! What an unhappy country! If everything is arranged on the same basis, you are far more barbarous than us.

The worthy chaplain tells us he spent the rest of the day touring the island and visiting the cabins. In the evening after supper father and mother besought him to sleep with their second daughter, and Palli presented herself in the same undress as Thia. Several times during the night he cried out "But my religion, but my calling," and the third night he was stirred by the same remorse with the eldest, Asto. The fourth night, as in honour bound, he consecrated to the wife of his host.

IV

Continuation of the Dialogue

A.: I respect this polite chaplain.

B.: And I rather the morals of the Tahitiens and the speech of Orou.

A.: Though a trifle European in style.

B.: Undoubtedly.

At this point the worthy chaplain regrets the shortness of his stay in Tahiti, and the difficulty of getting to know better the customs of a people sufficiently wise to stop of their own accord at mediocrity or lucky enough to enjoy a climate whose fertility guaranteed them a prolonged laziness, active enough to be beyond the absolute needs of life and indolent enough for their innocence, repose and felicity to have nothing to fear from a too rapid advance in knowledge. There nothing was condemned by public opinion or law, save what was condemned by nature. Village work and harvesting were done in common. The meaning attached to the word *property* was very restricted: the passion of love, by its reduction to a simple physical appetite, produced none of the disorders it does with us. The whole island presented the picture of a single large family and each cabin seemed more like different rooms in one of our big houses. He ended up by protesting that the Tahitiens will always be present in his memory, that he had been tempted to throw his clothes into the ship and pass the rest of his life among them; and that he is afraid of repenting more than once of not having done so.

A.: For all his eulogium, what conclusions can be usefully drawn from the morals and strange customs of an uncivilized people?

B.: I see that as soon as certain physical causes, as, for instance, the necessity of defeating an ungrateful soil, have brought out the intellectuality in man, this impulse carries him far beyond his goal, and once the limits of need passed, he is carried out into the boundless ocean of his phantasies from which he is never pulled back. May the lucky Tahitien stop where he is! For except in this distant nook of the globe, I perceive there never have been any morals and perhaps never will be anywhere.

A.: What do you mean, then, by morals?

B.: I mean general submission to, and conduct consequent on, laws good or bad. If the laws are good, morals are good. If the laws are bad, morals are bad. And if the laws, be they good or bad, are not observed, which is the worst of all social conditions, there are no morals at all. Then how do you wish laws to be observed when they are contradictory ? Run through the history of the centuries, of nations both ancient and modern, and you will find man in subjection to three codes, the natural code, the civil code, the religious code, and bound to infringe these three codes in turn, as they never agree. So it happens, as Orou guessed about ours, that in no country is there a natural man, a citizen or a pious person.

A.: From which you will doubtless conclude that if we base morals on the eternal relations subsisting between men, perhaps the religious law becomes unnecessary and the civil need only be the enunciation of the natural law.

B.: Certainly, unless we would multiply wicked men instead of making good ones.

A.: Or, if we must keep all three, the two last should be strict copies of the first, which we carry graved on the bottom of our hearts, and which will always be the stronger.

B.: That is not accurate. All we bring with us at birth is an organism like that of others, the same needs, a delight in the same pleasures, and a common aversion from the same pains. This is what makes up man as he is and should be the basis of a morality suited to him.

A.: That is far from easy.

B.: It is, in fact, so difficult that I would gladly believe the most savage nation in the world, the Tahitien, who has observed most strictly the natural law, to be nearer a satisfactory system of law than any civilized people.

A.: Because it is easier for the Tahitien to rid himself of his excessive rusticity than for us to turn back on our paces and reform our abuses.

B.: Especially those that relate to the union of the sexes.

A.: Perhaps. But let us begin at the beginning. Let us question nature frankly, and listen without partiality to the answer she will make on this point.

B.: Agreed.

A.: Is marriage natural ?

B.: If you mean by marriage the preference a female accords to one man above all the rest, or which one male accords to one female above all the rest, a mutual preference as a result of which there is formed a more or less lasting union, which perpetuates the species by the reproduction of individuals, yes, then marriage is natural.

A.: I agree with you. For this preference is observed not only in the human species but in other kinds of animal, as is witnessed by that large band of males who pursue the same female at springtime in the country, and only one of which gains the title of husband. What about gallantry ?

B.: If you mean by gallantry that variety of forceful or subtle devices inspired in either male or female by passion, which aims at obtaining the preference leading to the sweetest, the most important and the most widespread of pleasures, then gallantry is natural.

A.: I agree with you. It is attested by that diversity of prettinesses practised by the male to please the female, and by the female to stimulate the passion and fix the inclination of the male. And coquetry ?

B.: A lie, which consists in simulating a passion one does not feel and in promising a preference one will not grant. The male coquette plays with the female, the female coquette with the male, a treacherous game, entailing at times disastrous consequences, a ridiculous trickery for which deceiver and deceived are equally punished by the loss of the most precious moments of their lives.

A.: So according to you coquetry is not natural.

B.: I do not say that.

A.: And constancy ?

B.: I cannot improve on the words of Orou to the chaplain; it is the poor vanity of two children, who do not know themselves and are blinded by the intoxication of a moment to the instability of all around them.

A.: And fidelity, that rare phenomenon ?

B.: With us generally the obstinacy and self-torture of honest men and women: nothing in Tahiti.

A.: And jealousy ?

B.: The passion of a needy miserly animal in fear of want: an unjust feeling in men; the consequence of our bad morals, and of the right of property extended to a feeling, thinking, wishing, free being.

A.: So, according to you, jealousy is not natural.

B.: I do not say that. All vices and virtues are equally natural.

A.: The jealous man is gloomy.

B.: Like the tyrant, because he knows his fault.

A.: And modesty ?

B.: You are engaging me in a course of lectures on the code of gallantry. Man would rather not be either interrupted or distracted in the course of his pleasures. Those of love are followed by a weakness, which abandons him to the mercy of his enemy. That is all that can be natural in modesty. The rest is due to institutions.

The chaplain remarks in the third morsel, which I have not read you at all, that the Tahitien does not blush at those involuntary movements which are excited in him beside his wife and among his daughters: and that his daughters, when spectators of them, are sometimes much moved, never embarrassed. As soon as women became male property and the furtive enjoyment of a girl was considered a theft, we find the phrases *modesty*, *restraint*, *propriety* came into being, quite imaginary virtues and vices. In a word, society wished to raise up barriers between the two sexes which should prevent their inviting each other to violate the laws imposed on them, barriers which often produced the opposite effect by heating the imagination and stimulating desire. When I see trees planted round our great houses and a neck-piece which reveals part of a woman's neck, I seem to recognize a secret return towards the forest and an appeal to the first liberty of our former home. The Tahitien would say to us, "Why do you cover yourself up? What are you ashamed of? Are you doing wrong by yielding to the most august of natural impulses. Man, show yourself frankly, please. Woman, if this man suits you, receive him with equal frankness."

B.: There is no need to be angry. We may begin as civilized men: we nearly always finish as Tahitiens.

A.: But there is need. These conventional preliminaries take up half the time of a man of genius.

B.: But what does it matter as long as this pernicious impulse of the human spirit, against which you were crying out just now, is to-day considerably weakened? One of our present-day philosophers, asked why men courted women, not women men, answered it was natural to ask the person who could always give.

B.: That reasoning has always appeared to me more specious than solid. Nature, indecent if you will, inclines one sex without distinction towards the other. And when man is in the brutal savage state, which can be imagined, though it perhaps exists nowhere——

A.: Not even in Tahiti?

B.: No, the distance separating a man from a woman would be crossed by the most amorous. If they hang back, if they run away, if they pursue, if they avoid each other, if they attack, if they defend themselves, it is because passion, progressing at different rates, does not reside in them with equal force. So it happens that pleasure increases, is consumed and dies in the one, when it has hardly begun to operate in the other, and both parties are discontented. That is the faithful picture of what would occur between two young, free, and perfectly innocent beings. But when a woman has learnt by experience or education the more or less painful consequences of one sweet moment, her heart trembles at a man's approach. A man's heart does not tremble. His senses command and he obeys. A woman's senses explain and she fears to listen. It is the man's business to divert her from her fear, to intoxicate her and seduce her. Man retains all his natural impulse towards woman. The natural impulse of a woman towards a man varies, as a mathematician would say, directly as passion and inversely as fear, a ratio which is complicated by a multitude of diverse elements in our societies, elements which nearly all go to increase cowardice in one sex and length of pursuit in the other. It is a kind of tactic in which the resources of defence and the means of attack have developed on parallel lines. We have sanctified the resistance of the woman: we have attached disgrace to the violence of the man. Violence would be only a slight offence in Tahiti. It becomes a crime in our towns.

A.: But how has it come about that this act, so solemn in its object, and to which nature invites us by the most pressing of attractions, the greatest, the sweetest, and the most innocent of pleasures, has grown to be the most fruitful source of all our depravity and evil?

B.: Orou explained it a dozen times to the chaplain. Listen to him again and try to remember it.

By the tyranny of man, who has turned the possession of a woman into a right of property.

By manners and customs, which have overweighted the conjugal union with conditions.

By civil laws, which have subjected marriage to an infinity of formalities.

By the nature of our society, in which difference of rank and fortune have introduced the proper and improper.

By a strange contradiction, common to all existing societies, by which the birth of a child, which was always regarded as an increase of wealth for the nation, is now more often and more certainly an increase of poverty for the family.

By the political views of sovereigns, who have related everything to their own interest and safety.

By religious institutions, which have attached the names of vice and virtue to actions not susceptible to moral treatment.

How far we are from nature and happiness! The empire of nature cannot be destroyed. However much you handicap it with obstacles it will endure. Write as much as you please on tables of bronze (to use the expression of the wise Marcus Aurelius), that the pleasurable friction of two intestines is a crime, the heart of man will still be torn between the threats on your inscriptions and the violence of its own leanings. This untutored heart will not cease to cry out, and a hundred times in the course of life your terrifying inscriptions will disappear before our eyes. Engrave upon marble: Thou shalt not eat the dodo or the gryphon: thou shalt only know thy wife: thou shalt not be the husband of thy sister; and do not forget to increase the punishment to suit the strangeness of the discipline. You will become cruel yourselves, but you will not succeed in changing my nature.

A.: How short the code of nations would be if it conformed rigidly to the law of nature. How many errors and vices man would be spared!

B.: Would you like an abridged account of almost all our wretchedness? Here it is. There existed a natural man. There was introduced into this man an artificial man: and a civil war, enduring the whole of life, arose in the cavern. Sometimes the natural man is the stronger, sometimes he is struck down by the moral and artificial man. In either case the poor monster is pulled about, pinched with tweezers, tortured, stretched on the wheel, ceaselessly groaning, ceaselessly unhappy, either because a false enthusiasm for glory transports and intoxicates him or because a false humiliation curbs and depresses him. But still there are some exceptional circumstances which restore man to his first simplicity.

A.: Wretchedness and sickness, two great exorcisers.

B.: You have named them right. And then what happens to all our conventional virtues! In wretchedness a man has no remorse, in sickness no woman is modest.

A.: I have observed it.

B.: There is another phenomenon which will not have escaped you either. The return of the moral, artificial man follows step by step the progress from the state of sickness to that of convalescence and from the state of convalescence to that of health. The moment the illness is over, the internal struggles begin again and the intruder is nearly always vanquished.

A.: That is true. I have myself experienced that the natural man, when convalescent, enjoys a vigour fatal to the artificial moral man. But finally tell me, ought we to civilize man or abandon him to instinct?

B.: Must I answer you straight?

A.: Yes.

B.: If you aspire to be a tyrant, civilize him. Poison him as best you can with a morality contrary to nature. Put every kind of hindrance in his path. Embarrass his movements with a thousand obstacles. Attach terrifying spectres to him. Perpetuate the war in the cavern and see to it that the natural man is always enchained there under the foot of the moral artificial man. Do you wish him to be happy and free? Then do not meddle in his affairs. There will be quite enough unforeseen accidents to lead him to knowledge and depravity. One thing you may always be sure of. These wise law-givers have moulded and fashioned you to what you are not in your interests but in their own. I appeal to all political, civil, and religious institutions. Look below the surface. And unless I am very much mistaken you will find the human race from century to century bent beneath the yoke it pleased a handful of rascals to impose on it. Mistrust the man who comes to bring order. Order is always a means of getting control of other people by embarrassing them: and the Calabrians are almost the only people who have not been tricked by the flattery of law-givers.

A.: And you like this anarchy in Calabria?

B.: I appeal to experience, and dare swear their barbarism is less vicious than our urbanity. How many small meannesses go to equal the atrocity of a few great crimes about which so much pother is made? I regard uncivilized men as a multitude of scattered and isolated springs. Naturally if two of these springs crashed together, one or other or both would break. To obviate their inconvenience, an individual of profound wisdom and sublime genius collected these springs and made a machine with them. And in this machine called Society all the springs were made to act and react on each other and wear themselves out unceasingly. And more were smashed in a day in a state of legislation than in a year in the anarchy of nature. But what a noise! What ruin! What an enormous destruction of small springs when two, three or four of these huge machines crashed violently into each other.

A.: So you would prefer a state of brutal savage nature?

B.: Really I cannot say. But this I know. Townsmen have several times been seen to strip themselves and return to the forest. The woods-man has never put on clothes and come to the town.

A.: It has often occurred to me that the total of good and bad was variable for each individual, but that the happiness or unhappiness of any animal species had its limit which could not be crossed, and that our efforts perhaps finally resulted in an equal quantity of drawbacks and advantages, as if we were harassing ourselves to increase the two sides of an equation, between which an eternal and necessary equality subsisted. However, I have no doubt that the average life of the civilized man is longer than that of the savage.

B.: But supposing the duration of a machine is no true measure of the exhaustion it endures, what then?

A.: I see that on the whole you would be inclined to believe men get more wicked and miserable the more they are civilized.

B.: I shall not visit all the countries of the universe. I merely warn you that you will find the lot of man happy only in Tahiti, and tolerable in but one corner of Europe. In the second case the governors, being suspicious and jealous of their security, are busy keeping man in what you call brutishness.

A.: At Venice, perhaps ?

B.: Why not ? You will not deny, at any rate, that nowhere is there less acquired knowledge, less artificial morality, and less imaginary vice and virtue.

A.: I never expected a eulogium of that government from you.

B.: I am not making one. I indicate to you a kind of compensation for servitude and one which all travellers have felt and praised.

A.: A poor compensation.

B.: Perhaps. The Greeks proscribed the man who added a chord to the lyre of Mercury.

A.: And that ordinance was a scathing satire on their first law-givers. It is the first chord that must be cut.

B.: You have grasped my meaning. Whenever there is a lyre there are chords. As soon as natural appetites are sophisticated, you may count on bad women.

A.: Like the Reymer.*

B.: And atrocious men.

A.: Like Gardeil.*

B.: And other people unfortunate for no reason.

A.: Like Tanié,* Mlle de La Chaux,* the Chevalier Desroches,* and Mme de la Carlière.*

Certainly it would be ridiculous to look in Tahiti for examples of the depravity of the two first, and of the misfortunes of the last three. What is to be done then ? Shall we return to nature ? Shall we submit to laws ?

B.: We will preach against insensate laws until they are reformed. And meanwhile we will submit to them. He who of his own authority infringes a bad law authorizes everyone else to infringe a good

* For all these unfortunate persons see Diderot: Ceci n'est pas con conte.

one. It is less inconvenient to be mad among madmen than to be wise all alone. Let us say to ourselves, let us cry out continually that shame, punishment, and disgrace have been attached to things innocent in themselves. But let us not do those things: for shame, punishment, and disgrace are the greatest of all evils. Imitate the worthy chaplain. Be a monk in France, a savage in Tahiti.

A.: Take on the dress of the country one is going to and keep that of the country where one is.

B.: And above all be honest and scrupulously sincere with fragile beings, who cannot make us happy without abandoning the most precious advantages our forms of society can offer. And that thick fog, what has happened to it ?

A.: It has fallen.

B.: So we shall still be able, after dinner, to go out or to stay at home, as we wish.

A.: That will depend, I think, rather on the ladies than on ourselves.

B.: Always the ladies! We cannot take a step without their running into us.

A.: Suppose we read them the conversation of Orou and the chaplain ?

B.: What do you think they would say ?

A.: I have no idea.

B.: And what would they think ?

A.: Very likely the opposite of what they said.

REGRETS FOR AN OLD DRESSING-GOWN

WHYEVER did I not keep it? It was just made for me and I was made for it. It followed every fold in my body without inconveniencing it. I was picturesque and handsome. The new one, stiff and starched, makes a mannequin of me. There was no call to which its good-nature did not lend itself. For poverty is nearly always busy. If a book were covered with dust, one of its flaps was ready as a duster. When the ink on my pen was thick and would not flow, its side was ready. You could see traced in long black stripes the frequent services it had rendered me. These long stripes announced me the man of letters, the writer, the toiler. At present I look like one of the idle rich: no one knows who I am.

Beneath its shelter I feared the clumsiness neither of a valet or myself, neither jets of fire nor the fall of water. I was absolute master of my old dressing-gown. I have become the slave of my new one.

The dragon who guarded the Golden Fleece was not more worried than I am. Care envelops me.

The passionate old man, who gave himself over hand and foot to the caprices, to the mercy of a young madcap, said from morning till night: "Where is my good, kind, old housekeeper? What demon possessed me the day I turned her out for this?" Then he weeps and sighs.

I do not weep. I do not sigh. But every moment I say: "Cursed be the man who invented the art of giving value to common stuff by dying it scarlet.

Cursed be the precious garment I revere. Where is my old, comfortable, convenient length of stuff?"

Friends, keep your old friends; friends, fear the touch of wealth. Let my example teach you. Poverty has its freedom, luxury its restraint.

O Diogenes, if thou sawest thy disciple in the sumptuous mantle of Aristippus, how thou wouldst laugh! O Aristippus, that sumptuous mantle was purchased by much baseness. What a contrast between thy soft, cringing, effeminate life and the free, strong life of the ragged cynic! I have left the tub where I was king to serve under a tyrant.

That is not all, my friend. Listen to the ravages of luxury, and the results that follow from it.

My old dressing-gown went with the other rags round it. A straw chair, a wooden table, a Bergamo tapestry, a plank of pinewood, which supported a few books, a few smoky prints without borders nailed at each corner to the tapestry. Between these prints a few plaster casts were hung which formed with my dressing-gown an indigence full of harmony.

Everything has been put out of tune. No more ensemble, no more unity, no more beauty.

A new barren housekeeper who succeeds in the presbytery, the wife who enters the widower's house, the minister who replaces a minister in disgrace, the Molinist bishop who gets hold of the diocese of the Jansenist bishop, cannot cause more trouble than the scarlet intruder has caused at home.

I can bear, without disgust, the sight of a peasant woman and that piece of coarse cloth which covers her head: that hair which falls thinly over her cheeks: those rags, all holes, which half clothe her: the poor, short petticoat which goes but over half her legs: those naked feet covered with mud do not offend me. It is the image of a calling I respect. It is the abstraction of disgraces inherent in a necessary and unfortunate condition which I pity. But my heart rebels, and despite the perfumed atmosphere that follows her, I turn away my steps, I divert my eyes from that courtesan whose headdress in *point d'Angleterre*, whose dirty silk stockings and worn-out shoes point out to me the misery of to-day united with the luxury of last night.

Such would my home have been had the imperious scarlet not put all in order.

I saw the Bergamo give up to a damask hanging the wall to which it had been so long attached.

Two prints were not without merit: the Falling of the Manna in the Wilderness by Poussin and Esther before Ahasuerus, by the same master. One was disgracefully driven off by an old man of Rubens—'twas the sad Esther. The fall of the manna was scattered by a storm of Vernet.*

The straw chair relegated to an antechamber by the leather armchair.

Homer, Virgil, Horace, Cicero relieved the feeble pine that bent beneath their weight. They were shut up in a marquetry cupboard, more worthy of themselves than me.

A great glass seized on my chimney mantel.

Those two pretty casts, which I owed to the friendship of Falconet and which he had repaired himself, made way for a crouching Venus. Modern clay smashed by ancient bronze.

The wooden table still disputed the ground, sheltered behind a heap of pamphlets and papers, piled up *pêle-mêle* which should long have sheltered it from the threatened insult. One day it met its fate; for all my laziness, pamphlets and papers got arranged in the shelves of a precious bureau.

Fatal instinct of propriety, delicate and ruinous tact, sublime taste, which changes, which displaces, which raises up, which casts down: which empties the strong-

* Claude Joseph Vernet, landscape painter, 1714–1789.

boxes of fathers: leaves daughters without a dowry and sons without education: which makes so many fine things and so many great evils: thou who substituted in my house the precious bureau for the wooden table; it is thou who bringest down nations. And it is thou who may one day bring my possessions on to the Pont Saint Michel; and the hoarse voice of the auctioneer will be heard crying: "Twenty pounds for a crouching Venus."

The empty space left between the shelf of my bureau and the Storm by Vernet was unsightly. So it was filled by a clock. And what a clock too! A clock worthy of Geoffrin,* a clock where gold and bronze contrasted.

There was a vacant corner beside my window. This corner asked for a secretaire and got it.

Another unpleasing empty space between the lid of the secretaire and the fine Rubens head was filled by two La Grénées.

Here is a Magdalene by the same master. There a sketch by de Vien or de Machy. For I also went in for sketches. And thus was the edifying redoubt of the philosopher transformed to the scandalous cabinet of the tax-gatherer. I even insulted the national distress.

Of my first mediocrity nothing but a rag carpet is left. This trumpery carpet hardly squares with my luxury, I know. But I have sworn and I swear (for the feet of Denis the philosopher will never tread a Savonnerie masterpiece) that I will keep this carpet as the peasant transported from his hut to the King's palace kept his sabots. When in the morning, clad in my sumptuous scarlet I enter my cabinet, if I lower my eyes I perceive my old rag-carpet. It recalls to me my former state, and pride is checked at the entrance of my heart.

* The wealthy husband of the famous Mme Geoffrin, who helped to finance the *Encyclopædia*.

No, my friend, no. I am not corrupted. My door is always open to the needy suppliant. He meets with the same affable treatment. I listen to him, I advise him, I help him, I pity him. My soul is not hardened, my head is not exalted. My back is as good and sound as ever: the same frank tone: the same sensibility. My luxury is of recent date and the poison has not worked as yet. But with time who knows what may happen? What may be expected from one who has forgotten wife and daughter, fallen into debt, stopped being husband and father, and who instead of putting by in his faithful strong-box a useful sum . . .?

Oh, holy prophet, raise your hands to heaven, pray for a soul in peril, say to God: "If Thou seest in Thy eternal decrees riches corrupting the heart of Denis, spare not the masterpieces he adores. Destroy them and restore him to his former poverty." And I, I shall say to Heaven on my side: "O God, I resign myself to the prayer of the holy prophet and Thy will. I abandon all to Thee, take all back: yes all, except the Vernet. But leave me the Vernet. It is not the painter, but Thou who hast made it! Respect the work of friendship and Thine own. Look at that lighthouse, look at that adjacent tower which rises to the right. Look at that old tree the winds have torn. What an imposing mass! Look, below that dark mass, at those rocks all covered in green. Thus Thy mighty hand hath formed them! Thus Thy benevolent hand hath clothed them! Look at that irregular terrace descending from the rocks' foot towards the sea. It is the image of those dilapidations Thou allowest time to effect on the solidest things in the world. Would Thy sun have lighted it otherwise? God! If Thou destroyest this work of art, men will say Thou art a jealous God. Have pity for the poor wretches scattered on that bank. Is it not enough Thou hast shown them the bottom of the abyss? Hast Thou saved them but to ruin them again? Hear the prayer of him who thanks Thee. Assist the efforts of him who collects the sad relics of his fortune. Close Thine ear to the imprecations of that raging man: alas! he dreamed of such a profitable home-coming. He had thought upon quiet and retirement. This was his last voyage. A hundred times on the way he had calculated on his fingers the real size of his fortune. He had thought out all his investments. Now behold him cheated of all his hopes. He has scarcely the wherewithal to cover his naked limbs. Be touched by the tenderness of that married pair. See the terror Thou hast inspired in that woman. She gives thanks for the harm Thou has not done her. Meanwhile the son, too young to understand the peril to which Thou hast exposed him, his father and his mother, attends to the faithful companion of his journey; he is fastening the collar of his dog. Spare the innocent! Look at that mother, newly escaped from the water with her husband; it is not for herself she trembled, but for her child. See how she clasps it to her bosom: see how she kisses it. O God, recognize the waters Thou hast created. Recognize them as they are when Thy breath stirs and when Thy hand appeases them. Recognize the sombre clouds Thou hast assembled and which it hath pleased Thee to disperse. Already they draw apart and retire; already the light of the day-star is reborn on the face of the waters. I prophecy a calm from that pink horizon. How far off that horizon is! It does not merge with the sea. The sky descends below it and seems to turn round the earth. Oh, finish clearing up that sky and restoring to the sea its calmness! Allow those sailors to put off their stranded boat: aid their labour, give them strength, and leave me my picture. Leave it me to be the scourge with which Thou chastiseth the vain man. I am no longer the one men come to visit and to hear. They come to admire Vernet in my house. The painter has humiliated the philosopher."

Oh, my friend, what a fine Vernet mine is! The subject is the end of storm, which has had no fatal consequences. The waves are still breaking: and the sky is covered with clouds: the sailors are at work on their stranded ship: the inhabitants run down from the neighbouring mountains. What intelligence this master has! He has only needed a few principal figures to render each circumstance of the moment he has chosen! How true that scene is! With what lightness, facility, and vigour it is all painted! I want to keep this witness to his friendship. I want my son-in-law to hand it on to his children, and his children to theirs, and they to the ones that come after them.

If you could only see the fine ensemble of this piece. How well everything harmonizes. How cunningly the effects are linked together. How everything is given its proper value without effort or strain: how misty are those mountains on the right. How handsome are those rocks and the buildings piled above them: how picturesque that tree is, how bright the high lights on that terrace! What modulations of light! How truly, vivaciously, naturally and livingly these figures are arranged! How interesting they are! How strongly they are painted, how finely they are drawn! How they stand out from the background. How huge the space is! How life-like that water, those clouds, that sky, that horizon! Here the background is dark, and the light is on the foreground, the opposite to the usual technique. Come and see my Vernet, but do not take it from me!

In time my debts will be paid, remorse will be appeased: and my enjoyment will be pure. But fear not that I shall be seized with a frenzy for piling up beautiful objects. The friends I had, I have them still:

and their number has not increased. Lais belongs to me, but not I to Lais. I am happy in her arms, but will gladly hand her over to anyone I like, if he could make her happier than I can. And to whisper a secret in your ear, this Lais, who sells herself so dear, has never cost me a farthing.

CONVERSATION OF A PHILOSOPHER WITH THE MARÉCHALE DE ——

I HAD some business or other with Maréchal de ——. I went to his house one morning. He was out. I was shown in to Madame la Maréchale. She is a charming woman, beautiful and pious as an angel: and she has a tone of voice and naïveté of speech which entirely suit her face. She was dressing. A chair is drawn up. I sit down and we talk. As a result of some observations on my part which edified and surprised her (for she holds that the man who denies the Blessed Trinity is a ruffian who will end on the gallows), she said to me:

Are you not M Crudeli ?

CRUDELI: Yes.

MARÉCHALE: The man who believes in nothing ?

CRUDELI: I am.

MARÉCHALE: But your morals are the same as a believer's.

CRUDELI: Why not, if that believer is an honest man ?

MARÉCHALE: And you put that morality into practice ?

CRUDELI: As well as I can.

MARÉCHALE: What! you do not steal, or kill, or pillage ?

CRUDELI: Very rarely.

MARÉCHALE: Then what do you get out of not believing ?

CRUDELI: Nothing; but does one believe in order to get something out of it ?

Maréchale: I do not know. But a little self-interest comes in useful both for this world and the next.

Crudeli: I am a little sorry for our poor human race, to be no better than that.

Maréchale: So you do not steal at all?

Crudeli: I promise you, not.

Maréchale: But if you are neither a thief nor an assassin, you must admit you are hardly consistent.

Crudeli: Why so?

Maréchale: Because I think if I had nothing to fear or to hope, after death, I should allow myself a good many little pleasures here below. I admit I lend to God at a stiff rate of interest.

Crudeli: So you think, perhaps.

Maréchale: It is not a matter of thinking. It is a fact.

Crudeli: But might one ask, What are those things you would allow yourself, if you did not believe?

Maréchale: One might not. They are only for my confessor's ears.

Crudeli: For my part, I never expect any return on my money.

Maréchale: All beggars are in that situation.

Crudeli: You would rather I were a usurer?

Maréchale: Why, yes. One can be as usurious with God as one pleases. He cannot be ruined. It is hardly delicate, I know. But what does that matter? As the essential thing is to get into Heaven either by cunning or by force, we must use every means, and neglect no source of profit. Alas! whatever we do, we shall get but scanty recognition compared with what we had looked for. And you, you look for nothing?

Crudeli: Nothing.

MARÉCHALE: But that is very sad. Agree then—you are either a rogue or a madman.

CRUDELI: But I cannot.

MARÉCHALE: But what motive can an unbeliever have for being good, unless he be mad?

CRUDELI: I shall tell you.

MARÉCHALE: I shall be most grateful.

CRUDELI: Do you not think a man can be born with a such happy disposition as to find real pleasure in doing good?

MARÉCHALE: I do.

CRUDELI: And that he may have received an excellent education, which will strengthen his natural leaning towards benevolence.

MARÉCHALE: Certainly.

CRUDELI: And that, in later life, experience may have convinced us that on the whole it is better for one's happiness in this world to be an honest man than a rogue.

MARÉCHALE: Why, yes. But how can he be an honest man, when evil principles united with the passions involve us in evil?

CRUDELI: By inconsistency. And is there anything commoner than inconsistency?

MARÉCHALE: Alas! Unfortunately not. We believe, yet every day we believe as though we did not.

CRUDELI: And without believing, one behaves very much as if one did.

MARÉCHALE: If you like. But what can be the harm in having one reason the more, religion, for doing good, and one reason the less, unbelief, for doing wrong?

CRUDELI: None, if religion were a motive for doing good and unbelief for doing wrong.

Maréchale: But can there be any doubt about it? What is the essence of religion but to check our vile corrupted nature, and that of unbelief but to abandon it to its own wickedness by relieving it of fear?

Crudeli: That is going to involve us in a long discussion.

Maréchale: What of that? The Maréchal will not be back for a bit. And we are better employed in rational discussion than in slandering our neighbours.

Crudeli: Then I must go back a little.

Maréchale: As far as you like, provided you make yourself understood.

Crudeli: If I do not, it will be entirely my fault.

Maréchale: That is very polite of you. But you must know I have hardly read anything but my Prayer Book, and I do almost nothing but study the Gospels and breed children.

Crudeli: Two duties you have admirably fulfilled.

Maréchale: As regards the children, yes. Here are six round me and in a few days you will be able to see a seventh on my knee. But begin.

Crudeli: Well. Is there any good in this world which has not got its drawbacks?

Maréchale: None.

Crudeli: And any evil which has not got its advantages?

Maréchale: None.

Crudeli: What then do you call a good or an evil?

Maréchale: An evil is that which has more drawbacks than advantages, and a good that which has more advantages than drawbacks.

Crudeli: I hope you will be good enough to remember your definition of good and evil?

Maréchale: I will. But do you call that a definition?

Crudeli: Yes.

Maréchale: Then it is philosophy?

Crudeli: And very good philosophy, too.

Maréchale: So I have made philosophy!

Crudeli: So you are convinced that religion has more advantages than drawbacks. Hence you call it a good?

Maréchale: Yes.

Crudeli: And for my part, I have no doubt your bailiff robs you a little less just before Easter than he does a few days afterwards, and that from time to time religion prevents a number of small evils and produces a number of small goods.

Maréchale: Little by little, that tots up.

Crudeli: But do you think that these poky little advantages make up adequately for the terrible ravages religion has caused in the past and will cause in the future? Remember it has created and now perpetuates the most violent national hatreds. No Mussulman but believes he is doing an action agreeable to God and the holy prophet in exterminating every Christian. And the Christians on their side are scarcely more tolerant. Think how it has created and still perpetuates in the same country divisions rarely suppressed without the shedding of blood. Our own history offers us examples all too recent and too tragic. Think how it has created and still perpetuates, in society between citizens, and in the family between relatives, the most violent and most lasting of hatreds. Christ said he had come to separate husband from wife, mother from children, brother from sister, friend from friend. And his prediction has been all too faithfully fulfilled.

Maréchale: These are abuses, not the essentials, of the thing.

Crudeli: It is, if abuses and essentials are inseparable.

Maréchale: And how can you demonstrate that religion and its abuses are inseparable?

Crudeli: Very easily. Suppose a misanthrope had set out to harm the human race, what could he have invented better than belief in an incomprehensible being about whom men should never agree and to whom they should attach more importance than to their own lives. Now is it possible to separate from the notion of a Divinity the most profound incomprehensibility and the greatest importance?

Maréchale: No.

Crudeli: Your conclusion, then?

Maréchale: My conclusion is that it is an idea which might well be disastrous, if lunatics got hold of it.

Crudeli: And you may add that lunatics always have been and always will be in the vast majority; and that the most dangerous lunatics are those made so by religion, and that the disturbers of society know how to make good use of them when occasion arises.

Maréchale: But we must have something with which to frighten men off those actions, which escape the severity of the laws. Destroy religion, and what will you put in its place?

Crudeli: And suppose I had nothing to put in its place, there would always be one terrible prejudice the less. Besides, in no century and with no nation have religious opinions been the basis of national morals. The gods adored by the ancient Greeks and Romans, the most virtuous of people, were the merest scum: a Jupiter who should have been burnt alive: a Venus fit for a reformatory: a Mercury who ought to be in a jail.

MARÉCHALE: So you think it does not matter at all whether we be Christians or pagans; that we should be none the worse for being pagans and are none the better for being Christians?

CRUDELI: Honestly, I am certain of it, unless we should be slightly merrier for being pagans.

MARÉCHALE: That cannot be.

CRUDELI: But are there any Christians? I have never seen one.

MARÉCHALE: And you say that to me?

CRUDELI: No, not to you, but to one of my neighbours, who is as honest and pious as you: who thinks herself a Christian in all sincerity just as you do.

MARÉCHALE: And you made her admit she was wrong?

CRUDELI: In a moment.

MARÉCHALE: And how?

CRUDELI: I opened a New Testament, which she had used a great deal, for it was very worn. I read her the Sermon on the Mount, and after each article I asked her—Do you do that? Or that? Or even that? I went one further. She is very beautiful, and although most good and pious, she is well aware of the fact. She has a very white skin, and although she does not attach any great importance to this slender merit, she does not mind it being praised. Her throat is as handsome as throat can be: and although she is very modest, she thinks it as well that this should be noticed.

MARÉCHALE: But if only herself and her husband know it?

CRUDELI: Certainly, I think her husband knows it better than anyone else. But for a woman who prides herself on being such a tremendous Christian this is not enough. I said to her: " Is it not written in the

Gospel that he who lusts after his neighbour's wife has committed adultery in his heart?"

Maréchale: And she answered Yes.

Crudeli: And I said: And is not adultery committed in the heart as surely damned as adultery of the most thoroughgoing kind?

Maréchale: And she answered Yes.

Crudeli: And I said: And if the man is damned for the adultery he has committed in his heart, what will be the fate of the woman who invites all those who come near her to commit this crime? This last question embarrassed her.

Maréchale: I understand; for she did not, very carefully, cover up this throat of hers, which is handsome as throat can be.

Crudeli: That is so. She replied it was a convention, as if anything were more conventional than to call oneself a Christian and not be one. And that also that one must not dress absurdly, as if there could be any comparison between a trifling little absurdity and one's eternal damnation, as well as the damnation of one's neighbour. And also that she was in the hands of her dressmaker, as if it were not better to change one's dressmaker than to throw over one's religion. And that it was the whim of her husband, as if a husband were sufficiently insensate to demand from his wife the forgetfulness of decency and duty, and as if a true Christian should push obedience to a preposterous husband to the point of sacrificing the will of God and despising the threats of her Redeemer.

Maréchale: I knew all those childish answers before you mentioned them. And perhaps I should have employed them like your neighbour. And we should both have been insincere. But what line did she take after your protest?

Crudeli: The day after our conversation (it was a festival of the Church), as I was going up to my room, my beautiful and pious neighbour was coming down, on the way to Mass.

Maréchale: Dressed as usual.

Crudeli: Dressed as usual. I smiled. She smiled. We passed each other without speaking. And she, an honest woman! a Christian! a pious woman! And after this sample, and one hundred thousand others exactly like it, what real influence can I allow religion to have on morals? Practically none, and so much the better.

Maréchale: What! so much the better?

Crudeli: Yes. If twenty thousand Parisians took it into their heads to base their conduct strictly on the Sermon on the Mount . . .

Maréchale: Well, there would be a few handsome throats better covered.

Crudeli: And so many lunatics that the commissioner of police would not know what to do with them: for our asylums would never hold them. There are two moralities in Inspired Books. One general and common to all nations and all religions, which is more or less observed: the other, peculiar to each nation and each religion in which people believe, which they preach in church and praise up at home, but which is not observed at all.

Maréchale: And to what is this preposterous state of affairs due?

Crudeli: To the impossibility of subjecting a nation to a rule which suits only a few melancholiacs, who have imposed it on their characters. It is with religious as with monastic institutions; they relax with time. They are lunacies which cannot hold out against the constant impulse of nature, which brings us back under her law. See to it that private good be so closely united to public good that a citizen can hardly harm society without harming himself. Promise virtue its reward, as you have promised wickedness its punishment. Let virtue lead to high offices of state, without distinction of faith, wherever virtue is to be found. Then you need only count on a small number of wicked men, who are involved in vice by a perversity of nature which nothing can correct. No. Temptation is too near: hell too far off. Look for nothing worth the attention of a wise law-giver from a system of fantastic opinions, which imposes only on children: which encourages crime by its convenient system of penances: which sends the guilty man to ask pardon of God for harm done to man, and which degrades the order of natural and moral duties by subordinating it to an order of imaginary duties.

MARECHALE: I do not follow.

CRUDELI: Let me explain. But I think I hear the Maréchal's carriage coming back just in time to prevent my saying something silly.

MARÉCHALE: Say it. I shall not understand you. I am an adept at understanding only what gives me pleasure.

CRUDELI: I went up to her and said quite low in her ear: "Ask the vicar of your parish, which of the two crimes is, in his opinion, the more heinous—to piss into a sacred vessel or to blacken the reputation of an honest woman. He will shudder with horror at the first, and the civil law, which scarcely notices calumny while punishing sacrilege with fire, will complete the confusion of ideas and the corruption of the intelligence."

MARÉCHALE: I know more than one woman who would never eat meat on a Friday and who . . . I was going to make my silly contribution. Go on.

CRUDELI: But I simply must speak to the Maréchal.

Maréchale: One moment more, and then we will go and see him together. I do not quite see how to answer you, but you have not made me change my opinion.

Crudeli: I did not set out to change it. It is with religion as with marriage. Marriage, which has wrecked so many lives, has made for your happiness and for that of the Maréchal. You have both of you done well to marry. Religion, which has made, does make, and will make so many men wicked, has made you better still: you do well to keep it. It is sweet to you to imagine beside you, and above your head, a great and powerful being who sees you walk upon the earth, and this idea strengthens your steps. Continue to be happy in this august guarantor of your thoughts, in this spectator, in this sublime model for your actions.

Maréchale: I see you have not got the proselytizing mania.

Crudeli: Not in the least.

Maréchale: I think the better of you for it.

Crudeli: I allow everyone to think as he pleases, provided I am allowed to think as I please. And then those who exist in order to free themselves from these prejudices are scarcely in need of being catechized.

Maréchale: Do you think man can get along without superstition?

Crudeli: Not as long as he remains ignorant and timid.

Maréchale: Well then, superstition for superstition, ours is as good as another.

Crudeli: I do not think so.

Maréchale: Now tell me sincerely. Does the idea of being nothing after death not distress you?

Crudeli: I would rather exist, though I do not know why a Being who has been once capable of making me wretched for no reason should not enjoy doing so twice.

Maréchale: But if, despite this drawback, the hope of a life to come appear to you consoling and sweet, why tear it from us?

Crudeli: I do not entertain this hope because desire for it has not blinded me to its hollowness; but I take it away from no one else. If anyone can believe they will see without eyes, hear without ears, think without a head, love without a heart, feel without senses, exist without being anywhere, and be something without place or size, very well.

Maréchale: But who made this world?

Crudeli: I ask you.

Maréchale: God.

Crudeli: And what is God?

Maréchale: A spirit.

Crudeli: And if a spirit makes matter, why should not matter make a spirit!

Maréchale: And why should it?

Crudeli: Because I see it do so every day. Do you believe animals have souls?

Maréchale: Certainly I do.

Crudeli: Could you tell me, for example, what happens to the soul of the Peruvian serpent, hung on the chimney and exposed to the smoke for two years together while it is drying?

Maréchale: How can it matter to me what happens to it?

Crudeli: So you do not know that this serpent, after being dried and smoked, is resuscitated and reborn?

Maréchale: I do not believe it for a moment.

Crudeli: Yet a very clever man, Bouguer,* asserts it.

* Inventor of the Heliometer. He accompanied La Condamine to Peru.

MARÉCHALE: Your clever man is a liar.

CRUDELI: But suppose he were telling the truth?

MARÉCHALE: I should get off with believing that animals are machines.

CRUDELI: And man, who is only a machine a little more perfected than any other. . . . But the Maréchal.

MARÉCHALE: One more question and it is the last. Does your unbelief leave you calm?

CRUDELI: As calm as it is possible to be.

MARÉCHALE: But suppose you were mistaken?

CRUDELI: Suppose I were?

MARÉCHALE: Suppose everything you believe false were true and you were damned. Monsieur Crudeli, it is a terrible thing to be damned. To burn through eternity. It is a long time.

CRUDELI: La Fontaine thought we should be as comfortable as fishes in water.

MARÉCHALE: Yes, yes, but your La Fontaine became very serious at the end, and I expect the same of you.

CRUDELI: I can answer for nothing when my brain has softened. But if I end with one of those illnesses which leave the dying man in possession of his powers, I shall be no more distressed at the expected moment than I am now.

MARÉCHALE: Your fearlessness amazes me.

CRUDELI: I am much more amazed at the fearlessness of the dying man who believes in a severe judge, in one who weighs our most secret thoughts, and in whose balance the justest man would be lost through vanity if he did not tremble to find himself too light. If this dying man could choose between being wiped out and going before this tribunal, I should be much more amazed by his fearlessness if he hesitated to choose the first: unless, indeed, he were more insensate than the companion of Saint Bruno or more intoxicated with his own merits than Bohola.

MARÉCHALE: I have read the account of the associate of Saint Bruno, but I have never heard of your Bohola.

CRUDELI: He was a Jesuit of the College at Pinsk in Lithuania, who left at his death a casket full of money with a note written and signed in his own hand.

MARÉCHALE: And the note?

CRUDELI: . . . was as follows: "I want my dear colleague, to whom I hand over this casket, to open it when I have performed miracles. The money inside will go to the expenses in connection with my beatification. I have added some authentic memoirs in confirmation of my virtues which will be useful to those engaged on writing my life."

MARÉCHALE: But it is a roaring farce.

CRUDELI: To me, yes; but not to you: your God has got no sense of humour.

MARÉCHALE: That is so.

CRUDELI: It is very easy to sin grievously against your law.

MARÉCHALE: I agree. It is.

CRUDELI: The justice that will decide your fate is very stern.

MARÉCHALE: True.

CRUDELI: And if you believe in the oracles of your creed, the number of the saved is small.

MARÉCHALE: Oh, I am no Jansenist: I look only at the bright side of the medal. In my eyes the blood of Jesus Christ has flowed far. I should think it very odd if the Devil, who never sacrificed his son, nevertheless got the lion's share.

CRUDELI: Do you damn Socrates, Phocion, Aristides, Cato, Trajan, Marcus Aurelius ?

MARÉCHALE: Gracious me, no! Only wild beasts can believe that. Saint Paul said everyone will be judged by his own law and Saint Paul is right.

CRUDELI: And by what law will the unbeliever be judged ?

MARÉCHALE: Your case is rather different. You are one of those cursed inhabitants of Corozaïn and Betzaïda who shut their eyes to the light that shone on them, and put wax in their ears so as not to hear the voice of reason which spoke to them.

CRUDELI: But these Corozaïnians and Betzaïdans were unique if they were free to believe or not to believe.

MARÉCHALE: They saw prodigies enough to have raised the price of sackcloth and ashes in Tyre and Sidon.

CRUDELI: These inhabitants of Tyre and Sidon were intelligent, the Corozaïnian and Betzaïdan mere fools. But is it for him who made them fools to punish them for their folly. Just now I related to you an actual occurrence. Now I want to tell you a story: A young Mexican . . . But the Maréchal ?

MARÉCHALE: I will send to find out if we can see him. Well then, your young Mexican ?

CRUDELI: Tired of his work, walked one day upon the seashore. He saw a plank with one end in the water and the other on the beach. He takes his seat on the plank; and turning his gaze on the huge space stretched out before him, said. " It is certain my grandmother is talking nonsense when she romances about some inhabitants or other who, God knows when, came here heaven knows where from, but from some country beyond the seas. Why, there is no commonsense in it. Cannot I see the sea merging in the sky ? And can I believe, against the evidence of my senses, an old story of unknown date, which everyone rearranges to suit himself, which is a mere farrago of preposterous incidents over which men eat their hearts out, and tear out the whites of their eyes." As he reasoned thus, the undulating waters rocked him on his plank and he fell asleep. As he sleeps, the wind gets up, the waves carry the barque away, and behold our young reasoner started on his voyage.

MARÉCHALE: Alas! that is just like us. We are each on his plank: the wind blows and the waves carry us away.

CRUDELI: He was already far from the mainland when he awoke. And who was mighty surprised to find himself on the open sea? Why, our young Mexican. And who was more surprised still? He again, when the sea seemed to merge in the sky on every side, now that he had lost sight of the beach where he had been walking only a moment before. Then he began to suspect that he might have been mistaken, and that if the wind continued in the same quarter he might be carried on shore, amongst those inhabitants of whom his mother had talked to him so often.

MARÉCHALE: But you say nothing about his agitation.

CRUDELI: He felt none. He said to himself: "What does that matter to me, as long as I get on shore? I have argued like a fool, certainly. But I was sincere with myself, and that is all that can be expected of me. If it be not a virtue to be intelligent, it is not a crime to be a fool." Meanwhile, the wind went on blowing, the man and the plank drifted along, and the unknown shore began to appear. He touches land, and there he is!

MARÉCHALE: We shall meet again there one day, M Crudeli.

CRUDELI: I sincerely hope so. Wherever it may be, I shall always be flattered to pay you my addresses. Scarcely had he left his plank and set foot on the sand when he perceived a venerable old man standing by his side. The Mexican asked him where he was and whom he had the honour of addressing. "I am the sovereign of the country," answered the old man. At once the young man prostrated himself. "Get up," said the old man; "you have denied my existence?" "I have." "And the existence of my empire?" "I have." "I forgive you that because you acted in good faith. But the rest of your thoughts and actions have not been equally innocent." Then the old man, who held him by the ear, recalled to him all the errors of his life. And at each article the young Mexican bowed his head and beat his breast and prayed for pardon. . . . There now. Put yourself a moment in the place of the old man and tell me what you would have done. Would you have taken this insensate young man by the hair and joyfully dragged him along the beach for ever?

MARÉCHALE: To tell you the truth, no.

CRUDELI: And if one of your six pretty children, after escaping from the paternal roof, and committing every conceivable sort of folly, came home repentant?

MARÉCHALE: I should run to meet him. I should clasp him in my arms and bathe him with my tears. But his father the Maréchal would not take the thing so lightly.

CRUDELI: The Maréchal is not a tiger.

MARÉCHALE: Far from it.

CRUDELI: He would make rather a scene about it. But he would forgive in the end.

MARÉCHALE: Certainly.

CRUDELI: Especially if he came to reflect that, before becoming the father of the child, he had known all that was going to happen to it, and that punishing him for his faults would be of no use to himself, the guilty one, or his brothers.

Marechale: The Maréchal and the old man are two different people.

Crudeli: You mean to say that the Maréchal is better than the old man?

Maréchale: Heaven forbid! I mean to say that if my notion of justice is not the same as the Maréchal's perhaps the notion of the Maréchal will not be the same as the old man's.

Crudeli: But you cannot have realized the consequences of that answer. Either the general definition applies equally to you, to the Maréchal, to me, to the young Mexican and the old man, or I can no longer say what is what, or how one pleases or displeases the old man.

We had reached this point when we were told that the Maréchal expected us. As I gave his wife my hand, she said: It is enough to make one's head go round, is it not?

Crudeli: Why, if one's head is a good one?

Maréchale: After all, the simplest course is to act on the assumption that the old man exists.

Crudeli: Even when one does not believe it?

Maréchale: And when one does believe it, not to rely too much on his good nature.

Crudeli: That is the safest way, if not the politest.

Maréchale: By the way, if you had to state your principles to the magistrates, would you make a clean breast of them?

Crudeli: I should do my best to hinder the magistrates performing a brutal act.

Maréchale: Oh, you coward! And if you were at the point of death, would you submit to the ceremonies of the Church?

Crudeli: I should not fail to do so.

Maréchale: Oh, you wretched hypocrite!

ON WOMEN

I LIKE Thomas: I respect the pride of his soul and the nobility of his character. He is a very clever man and a very good man: hence not an ordinary man. To judge by his *Dissertation on Women*, he has not sufficiently experienced a passion, which I value more for the pains for which it consoles us than for the pleasures it affords us. He has thought a great deal, but he has not felt enough. His brain has been agitated, but his heart has remained calm. I should have written with less impartiality and wisdom; but I should have discoursed with more interest and warmth about the only being in nature who returns us feeling for feeling and is happy in the happiness she gives us. Five or six pages of enthusiasm scattered through his book would have broken up the continuity of his delicate observations and made a charming work. But he wanted his book to be sexless; and unfortunately he has succeeded all too well. It is an hermaphrodite without the sinews of a man or the softness of a woman. However, few present-day writers could have written a book so full of erudition, reason, delicacy, style, and harmony. But there is not sufficient variety or enough of that suppleness ever ready to be turned on to the infinite variety of a being extreme in strength and weakness who has a heart attack at the sight of a mouse or a spider, and who can sometimes brave the greatest terrors in life. It is, above all, by their passionate love, their attacks of jealousy, their transports of maternal tenderness, the manner in which they share prevalent and popular frenzies that women astonish us: for they are beautiful as the seraphim of Klopstock, terrible as the devils of Milton. I have seen love, jealousy, superstition, and rage developed in women to a degree beyond the experience of man. The contrast between the violence of their gestures and the sweetness of their features render them hideous. They are all the more disfigured by it. The distractions of a busy, contentious life break into our passions. Woman broods over hers. Her passions are like a fixed point on which her idleness and the futility of her occupations keep her eye unceasingly fixed. This point can expand indefinitely. And a woman would only need the entire solitude to which her nature inclines her to go mad. Submission to a master she dislikes is a torture to her. I have seen a virtuous wife shiver with horror at her husband's approach. I have seen her plunge into a bath and never think herself properly cleansed from the soilure of her duty. This sort of repugnance is almost unknown with us. Our organ is more indulgent. Many women die without having experienced the extreme of pleasure. This sensation which I am willing to consider a passing attack of epilepsy is rare with them, but never fails to come when we call for it. The sovereign happiness escapes them in the arms of the man they adore. We experience it with an easy woman we dislike. Less mistresses of their sensations than we are, their reward is less prompt and certain. A hundred times their expectation is deceived. Their organism is just the opposite of ours. The motive force which in them calls out for pleasure is so delicate and the source of it so distant, that we need not be surprised if pleasure does not come at all or gets lost upon the way. If you hear a woman abuse love or a man of letters speak contemptuously of public applause, you may be sure the charms of the one are passing and the talents of the other failing. No man ever sat at Delphi on the Sacred Tripod. The Pythian rôle is suited to women only. Only a woman's brain can be sufficiently exalted seriously to sense the approach of a god, to rave, to tear her hair, to foam at the mouth, to cry: "I feel him, I feel him, here he is, the God": and to find the proper language. A hermit,* whose ideas boiled like his words, said to the hieresiarchs of his day: "Address yourself to women: they absorb quickly because they are ignorant: they expand easily because they are shallow: they remember long because they are obstinate." Impenetrable in dissimulation, cruel in vengeance, persevering in their schemes, unscrupulous in the methods they employ, animated by a profound and secret hatred of male despotism, they seem linked by a loose plot for domination, in a sort of league such as that which subsists between the priests of every country; they know the articles of their bond without its having to be first communicated to them. They are naturally inquisitive and wish to know everything, be it to use it or to abuse it. In times of revolution, their inquisitiveness prostitutes them to party leaders. He who understands them is their implacable foe. If you love them, they will destroy you: they will destroy themselves. If you thwart their ambitions, they feel in the bottom of their hearts what the poet has put into the mouth of Roxane:

> Malgré tout mon amour, si dans cette journée
> Il ne m'attache à lui par un juste hyménée :
> S'il ose alléguer une odieuse loì ;
> Quand je fais tout pour lui, s'il ne fait tout pour moi,
> Dès le même moment, sans songer si je l'aime
> Sans consulter enfin si je perds moi-même,
> J'abandonne l'ingrat et le laisse rentrer
> Dans l'état malheureux d'oû j'ai su le tirer †
>
> RACINE : *Bajazet*, Act I, Sc. iii.

---

* Saint Jerome.

† Despite all my love, if he does not fairly marry me to-day, if he dares allege an odious law against me : if when I do all for him, he does not do all for me ; at this very moment, without thinking whether I love him, without caring in fact if I ruin myself, I abandon the ungrateful wretch, and let him return to the miserable state from which I dragged him.

All women ought to know the lines another though less elegant poet has addressed to one of their sex:

> C'eſt ainsi que, toujours en proie à leur délire
> Vos pareilles ont eu soutenir leur empire,
> Vous n'aimâtes jamais : votre cœur insolent
> Tend bien moins à l'amour, qu'à subjuguer l'amant.
> Qu'on vous fasse régner, tout vous paraîtra juſte.
> Mais vous mépriseriez l'amant le plus auguſte,
> S'il ne sacrifiait au pouvoir de vos yeux
> Son honneur, son devoir, la juſtice, et les dieux.*
>
> CREBILLON PÈRE : *Catalina*, Act II, Sc. i.

They will simulate the intoxication of passion if they are greatly anxious to deceive you : they will experience an intoxication without forgetting themselves. The moment of concentration on their schemes will perhaps be that of their self-abandonment. They will force their way through to what they want better than us. Pride is more their vice than ours. A young Samoyed woman danced naked, dagger in hand. She appeared to ſtrike herself. But she avoided with such singular skill the blows she dealt herself that she had persuaded her compatriots that some god made her invulnerable. And so her person became sacred. Some European travellers were present at her religious dance: and though they were sure this woman was only a very cunning mountebank, she nevertheless deceived their eyes by the quickness of her movements. Next day they besought her to dance again. "No," she said, "I will not. The god does not wish it.

> * Thus comes it that to frenzy e'er a prey,
> Your likes have never failed t'uphold their sway.
> Love you cannot. Your insolence of heart
> To serfdom would confine the lover's part.
> That you may reign, no means will seem unjuſt,
> But you'd despise a love howe'er auguſt
> Should he not, to the puissance of your eyes,
> Gods, honour, duty, juſtice, sacrifice.

I should wound myself." They insisted. The natives joined their prayer to that of the Europeans. She danced. She was unmasked: she perceived it, and in an instant she was stretched on the ground, the dagger with which she was armed plunged into her entrails. "I foresaw," she said to those who came to assist her, "that the god did not wish it, and that I should wound myself." What surprises me is not that she should prefer death to shame, but that she should let herself be cured. And have we not seen, in our own days, one of those women who, with children's head-dresses, represented the infancy of the church, with her feet and hands nailed to a cross, her side pierced by a lance, still sustain her part in convulsions of pain, with the cold sweat pouring from her limbs, her eyes dark with the veil of death, and saying to the leader of this troop of fanatics not in a voice of agony: "Father, I wish to sleep," but with that of a child: "Daddy, I want to go to bye-bye"?* There are a hundred women for one man capable of this endurance and presence of mind. This same woman, or one of her companions, said to the young Dudoyer† whom she regarded tenderly as he extracted with pincers the two nails that pierced her feet: "God, who has granted us the gift of miracles, has not always allowed us that of saintliness." Mme de Staal was thrown into the Bastille with her mistress the Duchesse du Maine.‡ She perceived that Madame

* *Cf. Correspondance de Grimm*, 1761. The description by La Condamine of the Jansenist fanatics.

† Du Doyer de Gastel describes in Grimm's correspondence the Miracle of St John's Day, 1759.

‡ The Duchesse de Maine was implicated in the conspiracy of the Spanish Ambassador Cellamare (1718) the object of which was to overturn the Government of the Regent Orléans. The Duchesse du Maine was the grand-daughter of the Great Condé. The Duc du Maine was the eldest child of Louis XIV and Mme de Montespan, and under the inoperative will of Louis XIV was given the effective government of France during the minority of Louis XV (*cf. Mémoires de Mme de Staal*.

du Maine had confessed everything. At once she weeps, rolls on the ground, and exclaims: "Oh, my poor mistress has lost her head." Do not look for anything like that from a man. Woman has inside her an organ, subject to terrible spasms, which rules her and rouses up in her phantoms of every sort. In her delirium she goes back into her past and plunges forward into the future, both states being all the while present to her. All her extraordinary ideas spring from this organ, which is peculiar to her sex. A woman who was hysterical in youth becomes devout in old age: the woman who retains any considerable energy in old age was hysterical in youth. Her head still speaks the language of the senses, though the senses themselves are mute. Nothing is more closely related to hysteria than ecstacy, visions, prophecy, revelations, and fiery poetry. When the Prussian woman Karsh raises her eyes towards a heaven on fire with lightning, she sees God in the clouds. She sees him shaking with a flap of his black robe the lightnings that will strike the head of the impious one: she sees the head of the impious one. Meanwhile, the recluse in her cell feels herself raised to heaven; her soul melts into the bosom of the Deity: her essence is mingled with the divine essence: she faints: she dies: her breast rises and falls rapidly: her companions gather round her and cut the laces of the garments that strangle her. Night comes on: she hears the celestial choirs: her voice is joined in concert. Then she comes down again to earth: she speaks of ineffable joys. All listen. She is convinced and convincing. A woman dominated by hysteria experiences something infernal or divine. Sometimes she makes me shudder; I have seen and heard her carrying within herself the fury of a wild beast! How much she felt! How wonderfully she expressed it! Her words were not those of a mortal woman. Mme Guyon writes with unrivalled eloquence in her book *Torrents*.* Saint Theresa has said of devils, " How luckless they are: they do not love!" Quietism is the hypocrisy of the perverse man, the true religion of the tender woman. There was, however, a man of such honesty of character and such rare simplicity of morals that a gentlewoman could safely forget herself beside him and melt into God. But this man was unique and called Fénelon. It was a woman who walked barefoot with flowing hair through the streets of Alexandria, a torch in one hand and a bowl in the other, saying: " I would burn Heaven with this torch and put out Hell with this water, that Man might love God for himself alone." Such a part only suits a woman. But one word is sufficient to destroy this fiery imagination, this spirit one would have thought indomitable. A doctor said to the women of Bordeaux, who were tormented by terrible vapours, that they were threatened with the falling sickness. In an instant they were cured. A doctor shakes burning iron in the eyes of a troop of epileptic girls. In an instant they are cured. The magistrates of Miletus announced that the first woman to kill herself would be exposed, naked, in the public place: and the Milesian women are reconciled to life. Women are subject to epidemic attacks of ferocity. The example of one will involve a multitude. Only the first will be a criminal: the rest are ill. Oh, women, what extraordinary children you are! With a little pain and sensibility (Fie! M Thomas, why did you not let yourself go with these two qualities, which are quite familiar to you ?), what pity could you not have inspired in us, by showing us women, subjected as we are to the infirmities of childhood, more repressed and neglected in their education, abandoned to the same caprices of fate, with a more mobile soul, more delicate organs, and with none of that natural or acquired strength which fits us for our

* Published for the first time in 1702.

destiny: reduced to silence in maturity, subject to a discomfort which urges them to become wives and mothers: then sad, disturbed, melancholy, and, in addition, parents alarmed not only for the health and life of their child, but also for its character: for it is at this critical moment of discomfort that a girl becomes what she will remain all her life, penetrating or stupid, sad or gay, serious or frivolous, good or bad, deceiving or fulfilling her mother's hopes. For many a long year each moon will bring back the same discomfort. The moment has arrived which will free her from parental despotism: her imagination expands before a future full of empty visions: her heart swims in a secret joy. Thou art pleased, unhappy creature, to rejoice: time would unceasingly have weakened the tyranny thou leavest; time will unceasingly increase the tyranny to which thou art passing. A husband is chosen for her. She becomes a mother. Pregnancy is painful to almost all women. It is in suffering, at the peril of their lives, at the price of their charms, and often to the detriment of their health, that women give birth to children. The first home of the child, and the two reservoirs of its nourishment, the organs which particularize its sex, are subject to two incurable maladies. There is, perhaps, no joy comparable to that of the mother who looks on her first-born. But this pleasure is bought very dear. The father hands over the care of the boys to a hireling. The mother remains charged with the guardianship of the girls. Age advances. Beauty passes. The years of desertion, bad temper, and boredom arrive. By discomfort nature persuaded them to be mothers. By a long and dangerous illness she takes away from them the power. What is a woman then? Neglected by her husband, abandoned by her children, a nothing in society, religious observance is her one last resource. In almost all countries the cruelty of the civil law is at one against women with the cruelty of nature. They have been treated like imbecile children. In organized countries there is no vexation man cannot safely practise on woman. The only reprisal in her power is followed by a more or less marked contempt, which varies in proportion as society is more or less moral. A savage can practise every sort of vexation on his wife. Woman, unhappy in the town, is unhappier still in the depth of the forest. Listen to the speech of an Indian woman on the banks of the Orinoco,* and listen to it, if you can, without emotion. The Jesuit missionary Gumilla reproached her with letting the daughter she had just brought into the world die, by cutting her navel-string too short. "Would to God, Father," she said, "would to God that the moment my mother brought me into the world she had had enough love and compassion to spare her child all I have endured and shall go on enduring till the end of my days. Had my mother suffocated me at birth, I should be dead. But I should not have felt death and should have escaped the unhappiest of conditions. How much have I suffered! and who knows how much remains for me to suffer till my death? Picture to yourself, Father, the pains that lie in store for an Indian woman among the Indians. They accompany us into the fields with bow and arrow. But we, we go there burdened with a child hanging from the breast and with another that we carry in a basket. They go to kill a bird or catch a fish. But we till the earth: and after we have borne the toils of sowing, we bear all the toils of harvest. They return in the evening without any burden, while we bring home roots for them to eat and maize for them to drink. Once home, they go off for conversation with their friends, while we go and look for wood and water to prepare their supper. Having eaten, they go to sleep, while we pass most of

* See *Histoire naturelle, civile, et géographique de l'Orénoque* (1748).

the night grinding the maize and preparing them chica. What is the reward of our vigils? They swill their chica, and get drunk; and when drunk they drag us by the hair and trample us under-foot. Oh, Father, would to God my mother had suffocated me at birth. Thou knowest thyself if our complaints be just. I tell thee what thou seest for thyself every day. But our greatest unhappiness thou couldst not know. It is sad for the poor Indian woman to serve her husband like a slave, crushed with labour in the fields, deprived of rest at home. But it is horrible to see him, after twenty years, take another and younger wife, lacking in judgment. He becomes attached to her. She strikes us, she strikes our children, she orders us about, she treats us like servants; and at the slightest murmur that escapes us, the branch of a tree is raised. . . . Oh, Father, how wouldst thou have us tolerate this condition? What can an Indian woman do better than spare her child a slavery a thousand times worse than death? Would to God, Father, I repeat, that my mother had loved me enough to bury me at birth. My heart would have had less for which to suffer, and my eyes for which to weep!"

Woman, how I pity thee! There is only one compensation for your ills. And had I been lawgiver, perhaps you would have received it. Were you freed from all the bonds of slavery, you would have been sacred wherever you had appeared. . . . When we write of women, we must needs dip our pen in the rainbow and throw upon the paper the dust of butterflies' wings. Like the pilgrim's little dog, pearls must fall when we shake our paw. But no pearls fall from the paw of M Thomas. It is not enough, M Thomas, to talk and to talk well about women. Make me see them. Hang them up under my eyes like so many thermometers to register the smallest change in manners and customs. Fix, as justly and as impartially as you can, the prerogatives of man and woman. But remember that, owing to her lack of principles and power of reflection, nothing penetrates deeply into the comprehension of women: notions of justice, virtue, vice, goodness, or wickedness, float on the superficies of their soul. Remember that women have clung with all the energy of nature to amour propre and self-interest. More civilized than us externally, they have stayed simple savages within, all more or less Macchiavellian. The symbol of women in general is that of the Apocalypse, on whose front was written MYSTERY. Where there is a brazen wall for us, for them there is often but a cobweb. We have been asked if women understand friendship. There are women who are men and men who are women, and I admit that I will never make a friend of a man-woman. We have more intellect than women; women more instinct than we. The only thing they are taught is to carry well the fig-leaf they have received from their first ancestress. Everything said and repeated to them eighteen or nineteen years on end comes down to this: "My child, pay attention to your fig-leaf. Your fig-leaf is right; your fig-leaf is wrong"! A declaration is worth practically nothing with a nation prone to gallantry. Man and woman merely see in it a proposal for reciprocal enjoyment. Still, what does this phrase, "I love you," so lightly pronounced, so frivolously interpreted, really mean? It really means "I should be greatly obliged if you would sacrifice to me your innocence and your morals: if you would lose the respect you have for yourself and with which you are treated by others: if you would walk with eyes lowered in society, at least till libertinage has become a habit and you have thrown off modesty: if you would renounce every honest condition; if you would make your parents die of grief and afford me a moment's pleasure." Mothers, read these lines to your daughters.

It is a brief commentary on all the flattering speeches which will be made to them. You cannot warn them too early. So much importance has been attached to gallantry that apparently no virtue is left to her who has taken the plunge. It is with her as with the religious humbug and false priest, in whom unbelief is almost the badge of depravity. This great crime once committed, they can be shocked at nothing. We read in books, they in the great book of the world. Thus their ignorance leads them to receive truth promptly when it is offered. No authority holds them in thrall. Truth is always finding, at the door of our heads, a Plato, an Aristotle; an Epicurus, a Zeno standing as sentinels, and armed with pikes to repel her. Women are rarely systematic; they are always guided by the moment. Thomas says nothing of the advantages accruing to men of letters from the society of women. That is ungrateful of him. The soul of women is not more upright than our own, but decency does not permit them to speak with our frankness. So they have invented a delicate warbling by means of which we may say straightforwardly all we want, when we have been whistled into their dovecot. Women either keep silent, or, frequently, give the impression of not daring to say what they do say. We can easily see that Jean-Jacques has wasted a great deal of time at the feet of women, and that Marmontel has passed a great deal of it in their arms. We might easily suspect Thomas and D'Alembert of having been too virtuous. Women accustom us to discuss with charm and clearness the dryest and thorniest subjects. We talk to them unceasingly: we wish them to listen: we are afraid of tiring or boring them. Hence we develop a particular method of explaining ourselves easily which passes from conversation into style. When women have genius, I think their brand is more original than our own.